The Billboard Book of

ROCK
ARRANGING

The Billboard Book of

ROCK ARRANGING

MARK MICHAELS
WITH JACKSON BRAIDER

BLUE CLIFF EDITIONS

Billboard Books
An imprint of Watson-Guptill Publications
New York

Managing Editor: Jackson Braider
Interior Design: Margo Dittmer
Typesetting: Graphicomposition

First published 1990 by Billboard Books, an imprint of Watson-Guptill Publications, a division of BPI Communications, Inc., 1515 Broadway, New York, NY 10036

Library of Congress Cataloging-in-Publication Data

Michaels, Mark
    The Billboard book of rock arranging/by Mark Michaels with Jackson Braider.
        p. cm.
    "A Blue Cliff editions book"
    ISBN 0-8230-7537-0
        1. Arrangement (Music).   2. Rock music—Instruction and study.
    I. Braider, Jackson.   II. Title
    MT86.M52   1990
    781.66'137—dc20   90-127
                                                                         CIP
    ISBN 0-8230-7537-0   MN

Manufactured in the United States of America

First printing 1990

1   2   3   4   5   6   7   8   9/95   94   93   92   91   90

Dedicated to the memory of Lillian N. Michaels

Acknowledgements

Thanks to Jackson Braider for his protean editorial skills, to Jason Schulman, Tad Lathrop, Mike Fink, Steve Tarshis, Larry Saltzman, Ken Hamberg, Mat Goldberg, Jack Freudenheim, Lenny Battapaglia, Jeff Pollack, Dan Axelrod, Al Ramos and mostly, to my wife Kathy, for her unwavering love, patience and understanding.

"Forget yourself. Become one with the universe and your music. Let it flow through you. No matter how perfect technically, if your expression is not natural and unselfconscious, it won't affect others emotionally."

—Basho

Table of Contents

PREFACE.. **9**
    by Artie Traum

PART I
The Art of Arranging

CHAPTER 1: *You Mean It Doesn't Just Happen?* **13**
    Styles and Intuitive Arrangements—The Group Effort—
    What This Book Is About

CHAPTER 2: *The Rudiments Of Music*............................. **33**
    The Musical Score—Notation as Illustration of Musical
    Practice—Explanation of Notation Techniques and Elements

CHAPTER 3: *How Arrangements Can Change A Song*........ **52**
    Introduction to the Aesthetics of the Arrangement
    (Economy, Balance, Variety, Focus)—Comparing Different
    Arrangements of a Song

CHAPTER 4: *Who Does The Arranging?*............................. **73**
    A Description of the Act of Arranging in the Performance
    of a Song—The Arranger as Producer, A & R Person,
    Engineer, Independent Agent, and Interpreter

PART II
Clothing the Beast

CHAPTER 5: *Arranging Rock Styles* **83**

CHAPTER 6: *The Blues Arrangement* **90**
    History—Blues Forms—Bass and Drum Parts—Guitar
    Accompaniments

CHAPTER 7: *The Rock And Rhythm 'n' Blues Arrangement* 112

History—Rock Styles from Rock 'n' Roll to Rhythm 'n' Blues, including Early Rock, Rockabilly, '60s Pop, and Soul

CHAPTER 8: *The Funk Arrangement* 126

Background—Prince and Tom Jones—Disco: The Ubiquitous Bass and Drum Parts, Guitar Accompaniments—Arranging for Reggae (Skank) Band

CHAPTER 9: *The Hard Rock Arrangement* 141

Hard Rock and Heavy Metal Style—Bass and Drum Parts—Creating a Hard Rock Arrangement

CHAPTER 10: *The Folk Arrangement* 152

The Acoustic Guitar—The Focus of the Acoustic Guitar in the Folk-Rock Arrangement—The Emergence of Third World Musics

PART III

Dressing in Style

CHAPTER 11: *MIDI And The Arranger* 161

by Ken Hamberg

History of the Synthesizer—The Synthesizer as Substitute for Live Instruments—Using MIDI for Arranging and Recording— Hardware and Software Options

APPENDIX 181

More Rudiments of Music and MIDI

SUGGESTED READING 189

Preface

Rock 'n' roll started in the garage. On streetcorners. In smoky bars. At the beach. In funky, rundown tenements. It was spontaneous music. Music with no arranger. Early rock 'n' roll was a monster created, literally, in the basement. The body of music moved, inexplicably, without a head. It rumbled across the world and conquered/liberated everyone in its path.

Rock was strummed, plucked, slammed, beaten, hummed, shouted, screamed and cried. Rock 'n' roll was gut music. You heard it and you laughed, or sobbed, or got mad. Rock 'n' roll "arranging" was an oxymoron. No one considered arranging it. Who would dare try to clothe that beast? Think about this: at the time that Chuck Berry, Buddy Holly, Little Richard, Bill Haley, the Shirelles and the Beatles went into gear, America had been listening to the "legit" music of big bands, Broadway crooners and Hollywood soundtracks. It was slick. It was mushy. It had all of the lumbering gloss of a 1950 Oldsmobile.

Not that early Rock didn't have form. It did. Usually three chords, played in repetition, blues style. The drums accented the 2 and 4 of the measure, the bass thumped on every beat, and the rhythm guitar jangled off-beat chops. Crunch. Pause. Crunch. Thwap! It was a Chevy convertible in overdrive.

The sound was deliberately raucous. It evolved. And it evolved by trial and error. It was rare that someone sat at the piano with a score, tapping out the parts. The parts were played to fit a particular song, and after a lot of arguing, trial-and-error, laughter and tears, an "arrangement" was hammered out. You can hear that struggle—and that spontaneous energy—in the early songs of the Rolling Stones, the Yardbirds, the Grateful Dead.

But it didn't take long before the formality of arranging began to influence rock 'n' roll records. As rock progressed, the traditional musicianship and "criteria of arrangement" began to surface. Rock and roll came out of the cold; the pioneers and innovators who were "the rebels" began to search for sanctuary in the hallowed halls of traditional pop music and style. The arrangers began to dress the beast...

Although you can hear arrangers at work with the Supremes, Neil Sedaka and Dionne Warwick, *Sergeant Pepper* was the turning point. It was, arguably, the most important record in rock. The combination of George Martin's classical ear and the rough-hewn genius of the Beatles led to a record that transcended anything that had come before. It opened the doorway to multitrack brilliance and was a broad evolutionary leap to the future: tape loops, backwards guitars, string ensembles, orchestras, echo upon echo. . .

The irony is this: much of the rock of the eighties has made a complete and utter turnaround. It's slick, perfect, clean, clear and totally in-tune and in-time. Computer technology— MIDI, synthesizers, multi-track recording, sequencing, vocal tuners, post-production editing and assembling, mixing capabilities, guitar tuners—has changed the face of rock music forever. And although the rough-hewn, tough-edged sounds of the past may be fading under the assault of hi-tech, the spirit of rock stays alive and vibrant.

Why? That is what this book attempts to answer.

PART I

The Art of Arranging

1

You Mean It Doesn't Just Happen?

The scene is a mountain setting somewhere in the Appalachians: Four musicians are tuning up their instruments—a guitar, banjo, and fiddle—while the guy on the washtub bass is pulling a wad of tobacco from his pouch of Day's Work.

"Clyde, thump that thar gutbucket on the downbeat, and Sister, you come in playing the tune the second time 'round." With that, the boot stomps four solid beats on the barn floor and the music begins. They haven't rehearsed at all, but to hear them play, you'd think they had been working this material together all their lives—and in a sense, you'd be right.

Fifty years or so later, there are four young men huddled under the railroad tressel just at the edge of town. They are oblivious to the sounds of the city on this warm summer night, their mission taking them far away from their shabby surroundings and daily routines. As his first notes ring out and reverberate off the stone walls, the bass sets the tempo and rhythm of what is to follow. Without a word passing between them, the other singers fall in with their own parts, easily, joyously creating melody and harmony as they sing. They become the music and the music becomes them.

Is it magic? No. Telepathy? No, it's not that either. Though the effects are magical—people are reeling around the barn floor; the singers beneath the overpass feel the intoxication of their sweet harmony—this is what happens when musicians working together know what to do and simply do it. It's proof that the whole is greater than the sum of its parts; in short, it's the magic of musical arrangement.

How to arrange: that's the subject of this book. How to make the most of the instruments and musicians available to you, whether it's on stage or in the recording studio, to make the most of your song. What can you expect an instrument to do? Perhaps more important, what are the limitations of your instrumentation? Once you begin to understand questions like these, then you'll start to see that arranging for a group or an ensemble is a matter of drawing upon strength and capability—be it of the instrument or of the musician.

While learning about instruments and their places in the arrangement is essential to this art, much of the arrangement itself depends on the material you've got to work with—its style, its content. Songs tend to fit pretty easily into the styles we have come to know and love (rhythm 'n' blues, country, pop, and so on) through radio programming, record store layout, and the various *Billboard* charts, and the stylistic influences of a song tend to have a great deal to say about how we "hear" it even before we arrange it.

Consider the two examples above: the barn band and the guys singing under the bridge. Without even hearing what they are performing, we already have a pretty good idea of the styles they're working in. Let's face it: a guitar, banjo, fiddle, and washtub bass are not going to be playing rap music, no matter how far you try to stretch your imagination. And while the four singers under the bridge might be rapping, the chances are pretty good that they aren't singing an old rock standard like "Born To Be Wild," which depended so much on its distorted guitar opening to make its mark on the listener's imagination.

A traditional country folk band and a doo-wop group: both represent arrangement in its most fundamental sense. The conventions of the style in each case have been firmly established through continuity and familiarity. The washtub bass player in the country folk band knows that his role is to "thump" on the first beat of the measure. And since this kind of music is usually played in 2/4 time, this sounds very much like a bass hitting on the first and third beats of each measure in 4/4 time. And the fiddle player knows to come in the second time around, because it gives more weight to the melody in its repetition, though the player may simply think that it "just sounds right that way." The guitar and banjo add the chordal accompaniment or the "inner voices" when the fiddle takes it place at the top.

In a similar vein, the various members of the doo-wop group know what they are supposed to do; they know what roles they play in the conventions of their style. The bass voice propels the ensemble; the lead—the upper voice—carries the melody. The other voices add the harmonic color.

Just because these two very different groups aren't working with charts, just because there is a certain informality in how they approach their respective songs, that doesn't mean that they aren't working with arrangements. The detailed roadmap of what each player is supposed to do is as firmly etched on their brains as the way home.

These two diverse examples show us how today's rock music draws its roots from rhythm 'n' blues and country/folk traditions as well as from other genres and styles. Conceptualizing, communicating, and creating the overall sound of a musical performance does not necessarily involve writing and using a *chart* .

But whether there are charts or not, music must always be arranged. We said that the task of the arranger is to make the most of what's available to him. Let's take that further and define an arrangement as that which determines the voices, instruments, harmonic structure (more on this later), rhythm, form, style, and tempo of a song or composition.

With this in mind, take a closer look at the doo-wop group: The first voice to enter singing in the doo-wop group is the bass, which is the lowest in terms of pitch or frequency. In other words, the role of the bass in the arrangement is to define the key of the song, its meter, and its tempo. Usually, the bass sounds on the first and third beats of the 4/4 measure (though this is not the case in reggae and African musics, as we will see later on in the book). Without the bass, the arrangement will fall apart. The finger-pop or snap which invariably accompanies on the second and fourth beats of the measure sets up a backbeat, helping to establish a stronger sense of a "groove."

Since the street-corner singers have already decided that they will be doing "In The Thrill Of The Night," the middle two voices enter together, singing the line "shaddup an' shove it up" in harmony. How do they know which two notes will sound "harmonized" when sung together? For that, they use the greatest musical tool they have for creating and arranging: the ear.

While we will discuss why certain sounds go together when others will not in the course of this book, the point here is that the interest created by the bass voice is immediately enhanced by two things: the chordal sound of three voices singing together and the counter-rhythm set up by the two middle voices and accentuated by the fingersnaps.

Then the lead singer enters, singing much higher than the others. The center of interest, which started with the bass and its rhythm, has shifted first to the harmony and come finally to rest with the lead, the melody of the song. With all the parts going—the bass and the accompanying harmonies, the rhythm and the counter-rhythm—the "groove" is in place. Feet start to move and the dance begins.

This same general means of creating an off-the-cuff arrangement is used throughout all popular and folk musics, including rock. The bassline/chords/melody/rhythm approach only changes in terms of the specific style.

In this scenario, the musical concepts of style, parts for each player and instruments used are all wedded together. The tempo and form are communicated verbally before or during the performance. How many times might you hear the Godfather of Soul, Mr. James Brown, direct his musicians to "go to the bridge?" So many times, in fact, that this spontaneous arranging has been parodied by Led Zeppelin in their tune "The Crunge."

Does this mean that James Brown has no need for and has never hired an arranger? On the contrary: When there is a large group of musicians, such as James Brown's big band, the players have to know who is playing what at which time. The basic arrangement in terms of form, tempo, rhythm, chords, bassline and single-line melody can be conveyed easily to the rhythm section players (bass, drums, piano, guitar, and a solo horn player), but what do the other dozen or so musicians play?

Enter the arranger—the guy who draws up the charts.

It should come as no surprise to anyone who listens to a range of popular music that the sounds and styles of rock, jazz, country, rhythm 'n' blues and modern classical music are mingling. The term "jazz fusion" is just one example of this merging of styles. While that has become something of a specialty, the contemporary arranger should be familiar with all of the current styles so that he or she may choose the appropriate tools (instrumentation, tempo, dynamics, form, harmony, rhythm, etc.) with which to work in creating a certain arrangement.

First, there is the matter of instrumentation. The style or genre generally dictates the kind of instrumentation used. For example, most bands playing rock, heavy metal, country, and rhythm 'n' blues all use a core of instruments common to all "rock" styles: drums, bass and two guitars. What might be added to this core in each of these different genres is electric piano (rock, rhythm 'n' blues), acoustic piano (country), mandolin and/or fiddle (country), saxophone (rock, R&B). The combinations of various instruments, particularly with the advent of advanced recording techniques, the commingling of musical styles, and the increasing sophistication of the synthesizer, has become limitless. But in the main, any of the core ensembles described above can fulfill the needs of the arranger working in those styles. This is because all of these rock genres musically support a vocal performance, and this lyric is the focus of the arrangement. The less vocal there is, the more interesting the arrangement must be to keep the listener's interest piqued. In a genre such as jazz, often having no vocalist, the focus is most often on the improvisatory talents of the individual musicians.

What are commonly called "bands" are, in the language of the arranger, "rhythm sections" with "vocalist(s)." By looking at rhythm sections as essentially "time sections," we can describe more accurately their function of creating the pulse or groove of the tune.

Let's create a rhythm section which will establish the groove, propel the song and keep the time, all the while leaving the players room to improvise their own patterns based on parts which are easy to play. If this sounds like what goes on during your band's rehearsal for performance or recording, then you have firsthand experience with arranging music—it's just that you haven't thought of your experience in those terms.

Our fictitious band will include a drummer, electric bassist, electric guitarist, acoustic guitarist, and keyboard player (who may play piano, organ, or synthesizer). As mentioned before, a group like this one is extremely versatile, its versatility being limited only by the creative and technical limitations of the individual players.

One of the band members (the acoustic guitarist, to be exact) has just written a draft or sketch of a song. She arrives at rehearsal with a typewritten lyric sheet (this is not a normal band), the melody committed to memory and the basic guitar chords to accompany her new tune. The working title is "Save The Last One For Me." Here is the lyric:

> *Red strawberries all night long*
> *Eat three pints and I don't care*
> *Do it upside down 'till they fall in your hair but*
> *Save the Last One for Me.*
>
> *Big bananas, yellow gold*
> *Look good cut in Jell-O mold*
> *Eat them 'till you drop or your stomach turns green but*
> *Save the Last One for Me.*

The singer/songwriter, whom we will call Fruithead (the names here have been changed to protect the guilty), sits everybody down and plays the tune. There is no introduction, and she sings the two verses in order without any musical break or interlude. Her musical cohorts like the melody, but there is no sense of rhythm to the music as Fruithead is just "strumming" chords, one strum for each beat of each measure, on 1, 2, 3, and 4. Wild applause answers her final chord: the guys have always liked sensitive poetry.

Fruithead asks her mates what they really think of her latest creation. Kong, the drummer, replies, "It's all right, but, uh, what kind of song is it?" What the eloquent Kong really wants to know is what drum beat the song requires. In the past, the band has usually come up with informal arrangements on their own, through a cooperative effort based on discussion, trial and error, yelling, screaming, and throwing various musical instruments at one another. This time, though, they turn to Fruithead for guidance. As the songwriter, she has become the de-facto arranger for "Save The Last One For Me."

"Kong, it's a hard rock tune. I want real heavy drums."

This seems to be just what Kong wanted to hear, and he reaches for his stickbag to find his heaviest drumsticks—the aluminum ones with steel tips. Fruithead shows the chords to the electric guitarist and keyboardist as the bassist listens in and writes out a simple chord chart. Here is what she writes:

Example 1:

This "chord chart" shows which chords are played, but there is nothing here to tell us when they are to be played. This kind of notation makes no reference to the time signature of the song. And since we haven't heard the song ourselves and since the music is not divided into measures by barlines, this chord sketch is essentially meaningless. A better way to express these chords would be like this:

Example 2:

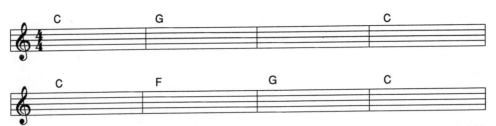

In 4/4 time, each measure or division represents four beats or counts of the music. The C chord is played for four beats, G for eight (two measures), C for eight, F for four, G for four, and finally C for four beats. This is only the starting point, though: what each musician will exactly play for the duration of each chord is still not specified—that for now is left to the discretion and imagination of the individual player.

Fruithead looks at the bassist's chord chart and says, "Let me add to this what I am playing on the acoustic." She takes the chord sketch and adds her part. The chart now looks like this:

Example 3:

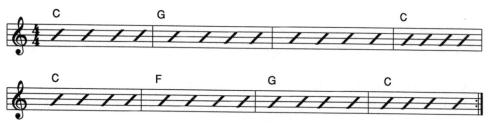

The angled slashes merely indicate one strum of the guitar on each beat of the measure. This is standard notation for rhythm guitar. The two dots at the end of the last measure tell us to go back to the beginning ("the top") and repeat. Since "Save The Last One For Me" has two verses and they are each sung over the identical chordal background, it's not necessary for us to write out the entire eight measures again. The repeat sign (:) is very common in music notation, but should not be used indiscriminately (more on this in the next chapter).

We have now entered the area of arranging known as orchestration—that is, the distribution of notes to the various instruments. The first task is to choose the instruments that go with the style. That's not actually an issue here because we are already dealing with Fruithead, Kong, and their band, who, as we have already decided, play the instruments most often used in a contemporary rhythm section.

Next order of business is to distribute the parts, the actual notes the respective—if not altogether respectable—musicians will play. Since the bass line should closely follow the movement of the chords, we see that the bassist will generally be playing a C note on the C chord, a G note on the G chord, and so on. This very simple approach to the bass is one of the hallmarks of the rock bassist. More inventive bassists (Paul McCartney, John Entwistle or Bill Wyman, for example) often play around chords rather than limit their playing to just the root or name of the chord. To begin with, our fictitious bassist will be playing only the root and "fifth" of each chord, and will be playing eight notes for each measure, in contrast to the four strums that Fruithead plays for each measure. If you don't know exactly what the "fifth" means, don't worry. The point here is that the bassist will be playing two different notes for each chord; one is the "tonic", the root note, while the other note will be another note in the chord. Here is what the first pass at the bass part might look like:

Example 4:

As you see, each measure contains eight notes, and even if you are not familiar with standard musical notation, it is clear that two notes in each measure are different from the other six.

Furthermore, the musical staff or palette goes from low to high in terms of pitch or frequency and therefore, one can see that those two different notes are lower in sound (deeper, bassier) that the other six. That is, the two different notes occupy a lower position on the staff and therefore sound lower to the human ear.

Let's look at Kong's drum part and see how it meshes with the bassline. Usually, the drums and bass set up the basic pulse or groove, so it's very important that the two parts relate and form a coherent rhythm. The listener should be able to hear the pulse by just listening to these two parts. Fruithead wants Kong to play something "heavy". This translates into having the drummer play a strong "backbeat" (the second and fourth beats in 4/4 time) on the snare against the basic impulse on downbeats one and three.

The use of the bass drum has become more predominant in recent years, stemming from rhythm 'n' blues (R&B) rhythm patterns. The bass drum part should "lock in" or be "in synch" with the bassline's rhythm and accents. When this happens, it has the effect of making the bass and bass drum sound as one, and this propels and strengthens the rhythm. You can hear this practice used to great effect in most of the Motown music of the 60's, in tunes such as "You Can't Hurry Love," "Ready For Love" and "The Way You Do The Things You Do."

Drum music is generally written with no designated pitch. A staff is not even necessary, but parts are written on manuscript paper with lines already printed. Commonly, the bass drum part is placed on the bottom space and the snare drum on the third space. Kong's "heavy" drumbeat (just bass drum and snare for now) would thus look like this:

Example 5:

Do you notice the squiggly lines above the numbered beats 1, 2, and 4? These are called "rests", moments of measured time where the part is not playing. The funny-looking thing on the bottom space (looks like a sick "7", doesn't it?) is also a rest. It tells the musician to rest for one-half of a beat while the squiggly one tells the musician to rest for one beat. The former is called an eighth rest and the latter a quarter rest, after the time value they occupy.

Don't let the word "rest" fool you. As we look at the rhythm of the bass and drum parts beat by beat, you'll see that there are moments when the bass isn't sounding, but the bass player is still playing—counting out in anticipation of the next attack. When we align one measure of the bass and drum parts, we'll see where they are playing together (on the same beat) and where they are not.

Example 6:

At first glance, it seems as if the drums and bass coincide on every numbered beat of the measure. They're both playing something on 1, 2, 3, and 4, but the "crack" or "pop" of the snare accents only beats 2 and 4, the backbeats. We have already spoken about the role of the bass in accenting beats 1 and 3 (remember the doo-wop bass singer?). By having the bass drum sound on those same beats, the effect is to intensify or accent the heavy bass part with a heavy bass drum.

Fruithead's drummer and bassist play this "groove" for a while to see how it works. She suggests having the bassist drop out on beats 2 and 4 so as to allow the snare drum to have more prominence—by sounding alone on the backbeats. Snare and bass drums add strength to ensemble accents, but one should use them discretely—it doesn't pay to overuse them. Fruithead knows this, and hearing it in the music, she intuits the change in feel resulting from the new bass part. The players accept her idea and now the combination of bass and drum parts looks like this, with Kong's hi-hat (double cymbal) part added in the top space of the staff as x's:

Example 7:

Melody is probably the most abstract of all elements in music, and yet it is also capable of being the most powerful. A strong melody can draw upon deep human emotions. In speaking of good tunes, musicians will talk about the line having a "nice contour"—that is, the melody goes up and down, resolving nicely and logically to the tonic, the main note of the key.

Back in the eighteenth century, one crazy Frenchman wanted to do an encyclopedia containing all possible melodies—he died without finishing it. And as yet, computer whizs haven't devised a program for creating beautiful melodies. One reason for this is that beauty remains in the ears of the listener. But the other and, perhaps, more important reason is the merest change can completely alter the impact of a melody—all of which might explain why, even after a thousand years of more-or-less tonal music, we are still able to write new and wonderful melodies.

The melody to "Save The Last One For Me" is not necessarily exquisite, though it's pleasant enough to listen to. It's hard to imagine a jewelry-laden matron of the arts clutching her hankie when she hears it, but Fruithead's melody is what it is, as you'll see below:

Example 8:

We certainly don't have much of a clue to the meaning of the lyric, though the guys in the band feel that it must be poetic. Still, the melody seems quite pleasant when sung, however, and it is not the point of this book to criticize melodies *per se.* After all, Fruithead has the right to compose any melody she wishes to, and we will defend her right to the death. It is to Fruithead's credit that she doesn't seem to be inhibited by fear of censure, clichés, or her own hangups. In any event, the phrases in her melody seem to follow one another in a way, so let's now turn to the parts that the electric (lead) guitarist and keyboardist (who happens to be playing a state-of-the-art synthesizer today) are going to be playing.

The lead guitarist suggests for himself an eighth-note pattern (remember that the bassist is playing a broken eighth-note pattern), accenting beats 2 and 4. His idea makes sense: The crack of the snare and the slash of the electric guitar occurring on the same beats should add quite a powerful backbeat to the music. And since the bassist has dropped out of the second and fourth beats, the guitar and drum parts should sound all the more dramatic.

The lead's eighth notes on all the beats of the measure help to propel the music. This kind of pattern is very common on modern rock tunes, often occurring in the work of such artists as the Cars, Bruce Springsteen and Robert Palmer. Fruithead likes this idea, since it goes along with her desire to have a real heavy, forceful sound in the new song. She suggests that the lead's eighth notes be played on the lower strings and that he do the accents on beats 2 and 4 on the high (treble) strings. He agrees, and proceeds to tune his instrument.

The arrangement is coming together well, and all without much recourse to a formal "arrangement" by someone outside the band. This impromptu "in-house" arrangement has already conveyed the style, the instruments used (orchestration), the parts the musicians will play (except for the keyboardist, and we'll talk about her next), the tempo (FAST!), the dynamics (there are none—the song is LOUD from start to finish), and the form (more on this later as well).

In a rhythm section, the role of the keyboard (be it piano, organ, or synth) is to reinforce the basic tonality and harmony established by the bass. The keyboard sets up rhythmic pulses of chord changes, but this "comping" (which comes from the word accompaniment) should not crowd or overpower the measure with too many chord formations, nor should the keyboardist totally wipe out the groove by sustaining chords too much. The keyboard chords should add interest to the music, and may accomplish this by providing tension harmonically (by playing notes outside the basic chords played by Fruithead on the acoustic), rhythmically (by playing notes or chords on different beats), or in both ways.

The keyboardist, Ivory, thinks that playing the same basic chords as Fruithead in a higher register (higher-sounding chords but with the same name as the guitar chords) will sound good on "Save The Last One For Me."

Since no one in the band is sustaining the chords—remember, all of the musicians are playing some kind of rhythmic pattern—Ivory wants to sustain the chords throughout the song. This means that she will play each chord on the first beat of the measure and keep her fingers down on that chord until a new chord change occurs in the music. This way, Ivory will be duplicating the harmonic structure of the arrangement without interfering with the rhythmic attack of the other instruments.

Everyone now has a pretty good idea of what their basic parts are, and the band is plugged in, tuned up and ready to play. The parts of all five musicians are notated below. Note that the keyboard requires two staves to fully convey its part—generally, the bottom staff is for the left or bass hand, while the upper staff is for the treble or right hand. Usually, the break between the staves occurs around middle C—the center note on keyboard.

Example 9:

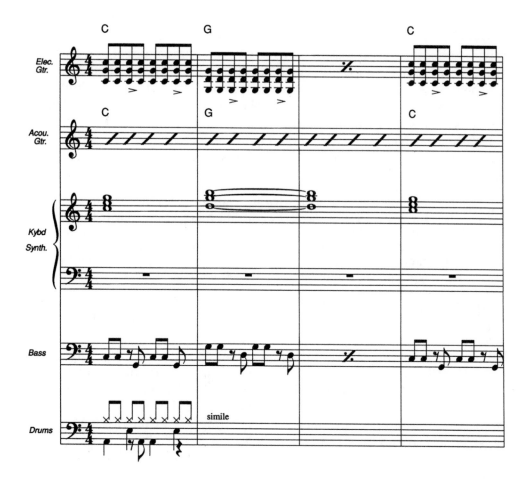

In the course of playing the song through, a few ideas have suggested themselves to the band on the matter of developing the song still further.

"Let's make an intro," Digit, the lead guitarist, exclaims. What he is thinking of is a rip-roaring mind-bending guitar line with super distortion and lots of signal processing (effects). True, the song does sound sort of boring in terms of its form or structure*. Digit suggests playing the chords "one time around" just like the verse.

---

*You can hear Example 9 as well as all of the other musical examples on the companion tapes to this book. See the ad in back for details.

Verse? We have now entered the territory of songwriting and arranging called "form." The verse is the portion of a song usually called the "A" part because the structure or form of the song is expressed by formulas like "A-A-B-A," "A-B-A," and so on. The form of "Save The Last..." is "A-A"—in other words, the musicians are playing the exact same musical part twice in succession.* In a sense, Digit is now co-writing the song, but that's acceptable here since in this band, all songwriting credit is shared anyway. Fruithead doesn't mind. So now they're about to play the song with a new "A" section added which will be the intro—music only, no vocals.

Here's what Nelson Riddle, noted arranger for Linda Ronstadt, Frank Sinatra, Nat "King" Cole, and others has to say about creating an introduction to a piece:

> I have found the best way to arrive at an appropriate intro is to dream up some sort of "catchy" phrase which fits the mood of the song to be arranged. If, in addition to using it as an intro, the same phrase can be restated from time to time during the arrangement...the subject of cohesion will be attended to in a most effective and original manner, and the singer can have his or her...first crack at the melody!

Though Digit hasn't yet heard of Nelson Riddle, when he plays his intro solo, Digit's notes seem to follow the shape of the vocal line (the melody).

Rather than taking a "catchy" intro and repeating it at some time during the song, Digit is doing somewhat the opposite. He is quoting or borrowing from the melody—in this case, following its shape or contour. His intro line looks like the example below. The wavy line over the last note means vibrato, a pulsating effect produced by the string player moving his or her finger either up and down or side to side.

Example 10:

*Consult *The Billboard Book of Songwriting* for more detailed discussions of form as it relates to songwriting.

It's important to understand what we mean by following the shape of the melody, though we will return to this concept later on. All of the arts, including music, reflect nature and the rhythms of the universe. Atoms, planets, stars, guitar strings, speaker cones, cymbals, drumheads, and eardrums all vibrate or move in natural order, creating or responding to certain fixed rhythms.

Really, the entire universe is just swinging! And just as there are shapes or patterns in painting, sculpture, and dance, there are also shapes in music. One aspect of this is the form—in the case of the song, the building blocks, like the intro and the verse. In the matter of melody, the shape describes the way in which the tune begins—usually at the tonic or one of the notes in the tonic harmony—moves (either up or down or both), and returns home. The next two staves show how the contour of Fruithead's melody compares with that of Digit's guitar intro.

Example 11:

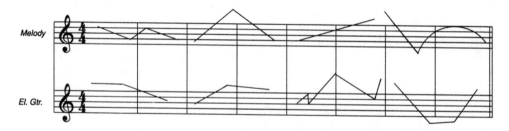

It appears that Fruithead's melody has indeed suggested an avenue of development for Digit's guitar intro. The most basic aspect of arranging in terms of emphasis is repetition, and we see that Digit has successfully repeated the shape of the melody in his playing. In addition, with this introduction, Digit has established continuity in the song. Continuity is important in arranging because it organizes and connects musical ideas. Arranger Adolph Sandole puts it this way:

> The music should grow out of itself, developing and with reference to previous material with controlled variety to hold the attention of the listener. All the elements of drama should be present. . .

Some of the elements alluded to are direction, motion, goal, climax, and dynamics. Fruithead likes the way the song sounds with the intro section and decides to write a middle section (sometimes called the "bridge" or "B part"). Her intuitive sense of arranging tells her that her song does not have movement towards a goal, to use some of the concepts presented above.

In the meantime, the synth player, Ivory, remarks that while she doesn't mind loud music—this is, after all, a rock band— this song is played at full-volume from beginning to end and she wonders how it would sound with some dynamics worked into the arrangement. So while Fruithead is busy composing the bridge, Ivory and the boys get together to discuss the dynamics (most simply, variations in volume and texture).

We have talked about how the drummer and bassist provide a pulse or groove. In addition to fulfilling this important role, the drummer can shape and define the various parts of the form and through his or her inventiveness. A drum fill before the chorus (there's no real chorus in "Save The Last..."), a change of beat or rhythm during the bridge, a huge cymbal crash on the final chord—such things all help to outline the music for both the players and listeners. Kong tells the band that the next time they play the song, he's going to add some fills before each "A" part or verse. He will also come down in volume after the guitar intro so that Fruithead's vocal entrance will be more dramatic. Lastly, he suggests that his musical mates pattern their dynamics after his. They agree.

Now Fruithead has returned, bearing the new bridge section of the tune in its initial form. The new chart that she has written out includes the intro section, verse, bridge, and verse in exactly that order. The song form is A-B-A (verse-bridge-verse) or A-A-B-A including the intro, which is the A part's chords played under the guitar line. Here is what the new bridge chords and melody look like on her chart:

Example 12:

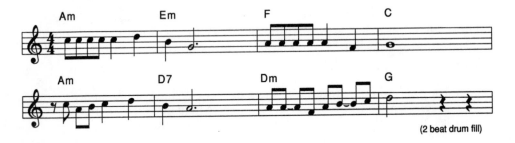

(2 beat drum fill)

Here is the lyric to be sung on this part:

I'm a modern fruithead person
Taking all that nature feeds
I want to be your food friend
Please share your apples with me

After playing the entire song, the musicians congratulate Fruithead on the bridge section. They like the new melody and the new chord changes—in short, they like the contrasts the bridge provides to the verse. The song now goes into a minor-sounding tonality in the bridge. The first chord is A minor, the "relative minor" of C major, the key of the song. The eight-bar bridge is divided into two phrases, each four measures long, and each of which begins with A minor.

It is a common practice in songwriting to set the bridge in a different key from the main part of the song. Most of the time, this key is related to the main key of the song—that is, the tonic chord in the new key will share notes with the tonic of the verse. We don't know if Fruithead is aware of this but she has certainly composed admirably.

However, as the band runs through the song with added bridge, Fruithead realizes that the overall sound is the same on the B section as it is on the verse. She feels that something has to be done with the instrumentation, the rhythm, and the dynamics on the bridge part and begins by making some specific suggestions to her fellow musicians.

"Kong, play half-time in the bridge and Digit, play big sustaining chords, like what Ivory was doing on the verse. I hear the bass playing very few notes in a rhythm that goes along with Kong's half-time feel. I'm gonna lay out [that means not play] and Ivory—uh—you fit in somewhere." It appears that Fruithead now has a very sure idea of what she wants and communicates her instructions pretty clearly.

Except for Ivory, the keyboardist, all of the musicians now have a framework to build upon, using their musical experience and creativity as the tools with the final criterion always being their ears—if it sounds right, it probably is right and therefore works within the arrangement.

"And everyone—play lower on the bridge! You know, that's a real sensitive part, where I'm talking about nature and being friends and all, and it really should come down there." Fruithead got her name because she writes songs about fruit, and to her, this is serious stuff (as a matter of fact, the name of the band is the Pits).

Before we get into the parts the musicians will be playing on the bridge, here are some of Elvis Costello's thoughts on arranging. They are very relevant to the process which is underway in our fictitious arrangement of "Save The Last One For Me." Elvis Costello talks about T-Bone Burnett's role as the co-producer of *King of America*:

> We cast the record together but he made all the suggestions and was like my interpreter for what was needed. There wasn't a tremendous amount of arrangement on that record. The songs were so simple, structurally, that it was pretty easy. . .to grab the right kind of feel, the right arrangements. The songs that didn't turn out so well, or didn't even make the record, were the ones that begged for more sophisticated, slightly fuller, more arranged sounds. . .we talked about sounds. . .he [Burnett] said "You should take that responsibility, otherwise it'll be the way I hear your songs, not the way you hear them."

To recap, what we'll now expect to be hearing on the bridge is half-time drums, big "sustainy" guitar chords, a bass part which fits with the half-time drums, and who-knows-what on the synthsizer. These are the sounds that Fruithead hears on the bridge to her tune. The half-time drum part which Kong has come up with looks like this when notated on the staff:

Example 13:

The four hits per measure on the "cymbal-bell" mean that Kong will be playing on the top of the cymbal where one gets a bell-like tone, rather than the "splashy" sound that comes from hitting the drumsticks on the edge of the cymbal. Note that his only snare accent comes on the fourth beat, while his bass drum rhythm remains the same as on the verse. A "half-time" feel has the effect of making the music sound slower, more spread out, due to the single snare accent. It feels like the music is moving "half as slowly"— thus the term "half-time." The bassist decides to strengthen this feel by placing his notes on the exact same beats as the drummer's bass drum part.

Digit, the electric lead guitarist, follows Fruithead's suggestion and gives his guitar the most sustained sound he can by manipulating his pickup selector switch, his guitar's tone controls and his foot-activated effects boxes. He turns on his reverb (which adds a spacey, echo-like dimension to his sound), his stereo chorus (which changes the sound of his six-string electric into that of a twelve-string) and his distortion booster (we all know what that means). He turns the tone on the guitar from treble to bass and uses his bass pickup—that is, the pickup located closest to the neck. All of this in the wink of an eye.

Now he is prepared for those thunderous chords, which will sustain for four beats (one measure) when slashed on the first beat of each measure.

Ivory has the idea that playing single notes on her synth might be a nice contrast to Digit's big chords. So, she will be playing out the notes in each chord, one at a time. This is known as an arpeggiated part (arpeggio is a musical term referring to playing the individual notes in a chord one at a time).

The band plays the entire tune and Fruithead is happy with the arrangement. The only additional change she makes is repeating the last two measures of the verse, during which she sings the "hook" or song title in this case, "Save The Last One For Me." This gives a sense of goal or finality to the arrangement—remember what we said earlier about repetition as an arranging tool. Repetition provides the musician and the listener some familiar ground as he or she plays and/or listens to a song. Everything from the riff to the verse is repeated in the popular song, and repetition, as one friend used to say, "is the mother of memory."

Lack of formal training as an arranger has not prevented Fruithead from successfully communicating her concepts to her band members, who likewise are not musically sophisticated. We have seen that by manipulating some basic facets of arranging such as orchestration, rhythm, dynamics, melody and form, she has created an "arrangement" from what was initially a song expressed solely by a rhythm guitar with a solo vocal.

When Elvis Costello was asked whether it was difficult to get his ideas across to some studio pros who played on his album *Spike*, he replied:

> When people start talking about particular intervals, using musical terminology, I might get a little lost. . .In the studio I hit things on piano, or sang parts I wanted to hear. . .they tolerated my. . .ignorance about things. . .this was just my way of working. . .

Like Fruithead, Elvis Costello arranged his material using an informal system of communicating ideas and concepts. Wouldn't it be easier to express oneself using a standardized system to which all musicians can relate, regardless of background, genre, and instrument? That is the goal of this book: to educate you, the musician, in the art and language of arranging. The informal, impromptu method of arranging will always be a viable path for arrangers working with less schooled musicians and for less schooled arrangers working with more sophisticated musicians (as in Elvis Costello's case above).

So that you may better understand the musical concepts and examples presented throughout the book, the next chapter will discuss rudiments of music, the fundamental principles to be learned about writing and reading music.

2

Rudiments of Music

Music: A Journey in Space and Time

One way to think of the musical chart is to look at it as a detailed roadmap, telling the player where he wants to go and how he is going to get there musically. Another way to look at standard musical notation (what most people simply call "written music") is graphically. The staff (the five parallel horizontal lines) serves as the time axis of the graph while the vertical placement of the notes on the staff, indicating their pitch or frequency, reflects their position in space.

In our discussion of the rudiments of music, we will be using a musical score—the collection of performance parts used by all the members of a group—to illustrate some of the basic concepts used in musical arranging. By looking at a score, you'll see how music is divided into units of time, how musicians see which pitches they are supposed to play, and you'll also see how the various parts are put together to make the performance you hear on the recording.

Somebody said one time that the musical score looks like a bunch of "hen scratches and fly specks," but once you begin to see what all these different markings mean, then you'll begin to get an idea of all the different things you have to think about when you start arranging songs for yourself. In one sense, it's a matter of intuition, but before you can do that, you have to know what you'll be working with.

The following example comes from Fruithead's immortal hit, "Save The Last One For Me." As you will see, it contains just about every single concept you'll need to know to get started on arranging. The circled letters refer to the various signs and symbols used in the score; you'll find their explanation below.

Example 14:

Save The Last One For Me

Words & Music By Mark Michaels

A. *The Staff*: Music is written by placing notes on the staff, which always has five lines and four spaces. Since there are so many instruments, each with its own range of notes from low to high, there aren't enough places on one staff to write all of the notes for all instruments. So, each instrument gets its own staff. When Fruithead's band goes into the studio to lay down this track, each member will get his or her own part, a piece of score which contains only the notes that he or she will play. Most parts only need one staff. Keyboard instruments get two—the top one for the right hand, the bottom for the left.

B. *Clefs* are signs found at the beginning of each staff which indicate two things: On the one hand, they tell you which line refers to which pitch; on the other, they tell you what register—the different ranges of notes from bass to treble—the pitches are in. So, though we use only one type of staff, its lines and spaces represent different notes, depending on which clef comes at the top.

The kind of charts we'll be dealing with use only the two most common clefs (there are four clefs all together): the treble or G clef and the bass or F clef. Various instruments read in different clefs: for example, the piccolo (the very high-pitched flute) uses the treble clef, while the bass uses the bass clef. The double staff of the keyboard will generally feature the treble clef for the right hand and the bass clef for the left.

Here are the treble and bass clefs, each placed on the staff, with middle C (the note in the exact middle of the piano keyboard) indicated on each. Also notated are the names of the lines and the spaces.

Example 15:

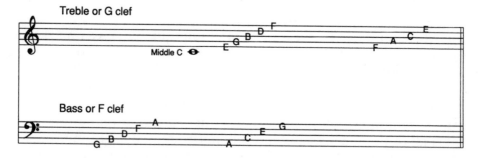

C. *Leger lines* are temporary extensions of the staff. This allows the copyist to write notes which are either too high or too low to fall on the lines and spaces of the staff itself.

D. The Time Signature (also called "meter"): This denotes the "time" of the piece—that is, the number of beats in a measure and the time value of the beat. The measure, marked off by bar lines, is the fundamental division of the song. So, when Dee Dee Ramone yells "one-two-three-four" at the start of a Ramones song, he is telling the band how the time of the song will be divided into what are called beats, and how long each one of those beats will last in time.

In other words, he is giving not only the time signature and the length of the measure in a song, he is also giving the tempo or speed of the song.

The time signature, which will be 4/4 throughout most of this book, tells one how many beats there are in each division or measure of the music/time. That's the top 4. The bottom 4 specifies which kind of note gets one beat—the quarter note in 4/4 time.

Perhaps a clearer example is waltz time, 3/4. The "one-two-three" reflects the number of beats in the measure; the 4 shows that the value of the beat is one quarter note.

E. Barlines are are thin lines, slightly thicker than note stems, which are used to separate measures on the staff. Measures are the basic unit of music/time, just as the familiar measures of pounds, ounces and grams are divisions of weight. Music written on a single staff doesn't require a bar line at the far left of the page, but double staff (piano, for example) music does. Furthermore, double staff notation requires a barline passing through both staffs, as is the case in this chart. Double barlines indicate the end of a section within a composition or, if drawn with a thicker second line, the end of a composition (not illustrated on the chart).

F., G., H., I., J. Notes: Various kinds of notes each represent a different duration of time. The most commonly used notes are whole (F), half (G), quarter (H), eighth (I) and sixteenth (J).

The whole note sounds for the length of four quarter notes (in 4/4 time, that's the equivalent of one measure). The half note sounds for two quarters or half a measure and so on. And just as the quarter note is a subdivision of the whole and the half notes, the quarter can itself be subdivided into eighths and sixteenths. If we want to count all of the eighth notes in one measure of 4/4 time, we would say "one-and-two-and-three-and-four-and." If we counted all of the sixteenth notes in one measure, we might say "one-ee-and-uh, two-ee-and-uh, three-ee-and-uh, four-ee-and-uh." It is better to count off the start of a song verbally with "one-two-three-four" or "one-and-two-and-three-and-four-and" than it is to rely on a purely instrumental count—that is, unless you have a monster timekeeper on your guitar or keyboard. Usually even a solo musical intro will be preceded by a verbal countoff.

We see that by the two factors of placement on the staff and selection of note symbol (open or solid) one can clearly express the pitch and duration of a musical note.

K. Beams are used to connect eighths and sixteenths to make reading easier. Here, the bassist's first measure contains beamed eighth notes, while the electric guitarist's fifth measure illustrates beamed sixteenth notes.

An important thing to remember about beams: music copyists say that beams cannot cross a beat. In other words, you shouldn't beam together an eighth note coming in the middle of a beat with a following eighth note that comes on the next beat. The reason is that you don't want to confuse the player as to where the beat falls in relation to the eighth note.

L., M., N., O., P. Rests: Each kind of note has a rest associated with it. Rests are timed periods of silence in music, and they last the same amount of time—the whole (L), half (M), quarter (N), eighth (O) and sixteenth rests (P)—as their corresponding notes.

Notes and rests are added up to give the full count of the measure. In 4/4 time, then, all of the must add up to the top 4 in 4/4 time, 3 in 3/4 time, and so on. The total of beats in the measure must always be there, unless the song has a downbeat at the very beginning, in which case, the very last measure will be shortened by the value of the material featured at the very top (I know this all sounds somewhat confusing, but believe me, it will all work out in the end).

Q., R. Altered time values of basic notes: There are two ways in which you can alter the time value of a note—the tie (Q) and the dot (R). In both cases, the alteration lengthens the value of the note it is attached to.

A tie is a curved line that joins two adjacent notes of the same pitch. It indicates that the first note is to be prolonged into the next note, and the next note is not to be played or struck anew. You can tie two (or more, in some special instances) notes within a measure or across barlines.

The other way to increase the duration of a particular note is to place a dot after the notehead. A dot following a note increases that note's value by one-half its original value. Thus, a dotted quarter is equal to a quarter note plus and eighth.

While dots and ties (it sounds a bit like fashion talk, doesn't it?) do the same basic thing—they both lengthen the value of a note—they have different applications in terms of written music. Generally, a dot cannot cross a beat, while that is all that ties do. You almost always write dotted notes on the beat and tied notes on the off-beat. You also tie notes over barlines.

Here's a good way to remember how they work: a dotted note will almost always be followed by a second note that is equal to the value of the dot. Thus, a dotted eighth (equal to an eighth plus a sixteenth) will be followed by a sixteenth note; a dotted quarter will similarly be followed by an eighth, and so on. In 4/4 time, you beam together a dotted eighth and a sixteenth.

Ties, on the other hand, will usually come up when you're dealing with syncopations—strong notes on the offbeat.

S. Accidentals: Just as you can change the time value of a note with a simple marking, you can also alter the pitch of any note by using a sharp (#) or flat (♭) sign. These are known as *accidentals* when they occur during a piece and they either raise or lower the pitch of a note by one half-step. A half-step is equal to an adjacent note on the keyboard or one fret on the guitar or bass. Accidentals only affect the note which they precede and notes of the same pitch and only within the measure.

Another accidental is called a natural (♮), and it cancels any preceding accidental in the measure. It, too, only affects the pitch to which it is applied, and has no affect on the same note in other octaves. The natural also lasts only for the duration of the measure in which it appears.

T. Tempo markings: Notes written on the staff only show the relative duration of sounds. The actual duration depends upon the speed or tempo at which the piece of music is played.

The tempo of a song can be expressed in two ways: by a metronome marking (such as mm=208, for example) or through the use of such terms as "slowly," "fast," and the like. A metronome is a pendulum apparatus (often an electrical clockwork nowadays) that clicks the beat with depressing regularity. That's why musicians practice with metronomes—so they can learn how to play in time.

Such words as "fast" or "lightly" also indicate tempo, but not a precisely as a metronome marking does. However, a metronome is not always handy at rehearsals or performances. Familiarity with the Italian terms traditionally used to express tempo is important, and you can find a list of them in the Appendix.

There is an increasing trend towards using the language of the origin of the music or composer for terms describing tempo, and in your music you will probably use tempo markings such as "rock ballad," "very fast," "slowly" and other similar terms which can be understood easily by most musicians.

Tempo markings and metronome markings are placed at the start of a composition, above the staff and aligned with the time signature.

U. A slur is a curved line unifying groups of notes to be played together in a smooth manner. Slurs should start and end of the center of the notes that begin and end the phrase. They look a bit like ties, but the difference is that they join groups of different pitches together.

V. Repeating marks: Rather than continuing to write out identical measures, the symbol for repeating the current measure is often used. In this case, the drummer would play the music (drumbeat) written out in the first two measures for the remaining six measures.

Repeat marks for a single beat repeat (slash marks) are placed within the body of the staff, as below:

Example 16:

W. Simile: Often a musician will be called upon to keep repeating the same rhythmic pattern. An acceptable shortcut is to use the word *simile*, which instructs the player to continue "in a similar manner."

X, Y. Chord symbols (X) are written above the staff. When a chord is to be played with a note in the bass other than its root (name) note, the bass note is placed below an oblique line, as in F/C (an F chord with a C note in the bass). Chords can also be written out on the staff (Y) to show particular voicing or the exact notes the arranger wants to hear.

Z. Key signatures (not marked): When sharps or flats appear on the staff by themselves in a group at the far left of the staff, right after the clef, they signify the key signature of the piece. The key signature simply tells the musician which notes, in all registers or octaves, are to be consistently sharped or flatted.

Each key signature refers to either a major or a minor key. Thus, four sharps at the far left of the staff tells you that the piece is in either E major (the four sharps are F#, G#, C#, and D#) or C# minor, which has the same sharped notes. The actual key usually depends on what the last note is in the bass.

Be aware that it is common for songs to change keys as it goes from one section to another—from the verse to the bridge, for example. So, remember that the key signature is only a guide; if you want to use a note that does not fit in with the key signature, that's when you bring in the accidentals. This is especially true if you're working in a minor key.

Repetition: The Mother of Memory

Repetition is such an important part of the modern song arrangement that it really needs to be discussed in some detail. Remember when we were describing the form of Fruithead's song— A-A-B-A? Each of those A's represents a repeated strain of the song, the verse. But that's not the only thing that is being repeated in this song. There is, for example, the drum beat established in the first measure, and the arpeggios in Ivory's keyboard part in the bridge—the B section.

Arrangers over the centuries have invented various bits of shorthand, ways of showing musicians what they should repeat in a performance and where they should do it. Many of these do not appear in the score above, so here are a few more "hen scratches and fly specks" to add to your burgeoning fund of musical knowledge—all of them having to do with repetition, the mother of memory. These can refer to as much as an entire verse or as little as a single measure.

Repeating sections of a piece use a repeat mark which is a thin line and a thick line with dots in the second and third spaces marked on the inside left of vertical lines. The first occasion in a song in which this kind of repeat mark is used usually takes one back to the beginning of the song, the top. In the following example, the musician would play the first four measures and then repeat them, for a total of eight measures.

Example 17:

If the repeat sign does not take you back to the top, as above, then it must direct you to where you go back, and this place in the music is signified by the reverse image of the same sign, the dots being placed on the righthand side of the vertical lines. In the next example, the players repeats the two measures which are encompassed by the two repeat signs facing one another.

Example 18:

The five measures thus actually become seven measures, so you can see how the repeat sign saves not only space but time as well. And it saves the musician some trouble, too. Remember, though, that the second time you face the repeat sign, you will ignore it as you have already carried out its initial command to repeat the section—once.

However, when a section to be repeated has a different conclusion, first and second endings are used. In following the examples below, think of first and second endings as being detours on the musical roadmap.

Example 19:

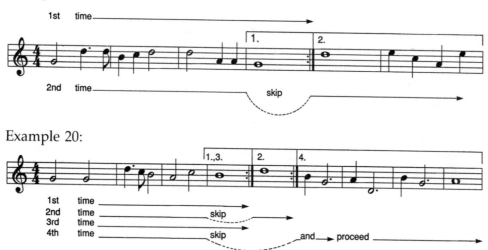

Example 20:

In playing the first example, the musician would play the first three measures and then play what is included under the first ending bracket as the fourth measure. Then, following the repeat sign instruction, one would go back to the top plays the first three measures again. The second time through, though, the musician skips the measure under the first ending bracket and plays what is under the second ending bracket before going onto the next section. So, we see that by using the first/second ending concept we have eliminated the need to re-write three measures of the same music. It's a good practice to examine your roadmap/chart first to check on your specified "travel plans," so you won't miss playing the music properly when you get to first and second endings and other directives.

If the music requires more different endings than first and second endings can provide, you can use as many different endings as the music requires. The second example actually shows four endings. The first and third endings are the same, so the bracket above reads "1., 3." The second time through, the musician plays the second ending—bracketed above and marked "2." On the fourth time, the fourth ending is used, at which point one goes on to play the rest of the music.

Now we'll walk through this example. As in the first example, play the first three measures and then what is under the first ending bracket. Repeat to the top, play the first three measures again but this time skip the ending marked "1.,3" (which is actually the first and third ending) and play the second ending. Go back to the top again, play the first three measures, and then play the third ending (same as the first ending). Repeat to the top, play the first three measures, skip the first, second, and third endings, and go directly to the fourth ending. Since there's no repeat under the fourth ending bracket, you would then proceed through the rest of the piece.

So you can get a sense of how much space we've saved, figure that the four times through the three measures means that you've actually played twelve measures; add to that the repeats of the first and third endings (fourteen so far) and the second and fourth endings. We've managed to fit sixteen measures of music, then, into six little bars.

Sometimes repetitions are not immediate. That is, the arranger may want you to back to another part of the song and play it again. This is where the concepts of *da capo* ("from the head") and *dal segno* ("from the sign") come into play.

Da capo, abbreviated "D.C.", directs the musician to go to the very beginning and start again. *Dal segno* ("D.S.") tells you to go back to the point at which you see the sign (𝄋) over the staff. Here are examples of both:

Example 21:

Example 22:

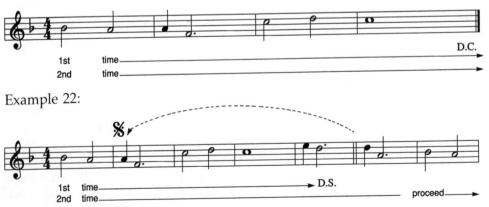

Two other words are often associated with the D.C. and D.S. repeats. They are *coda* and *fine* (pronounced "fee-nay"). *Coda* means "tail" and *fine* means "end." D.S. and D.C. are combined with the words coda and fine in the following ways:

> *D.C. al fine*: go to the beginning and play to the end.
> *D.C. al coda*: go to the beginning, play until the coda sign and then jump to the coda.
> *D.S. al fine*: go to the sign and play to the end.
> *D.S. al coda*: go to the sign, play until the coda sign and then jump to the coda.

Here are examples of the four different musical instructions described above:

Example 23:

Example 24:

Example 25:

Example 26:

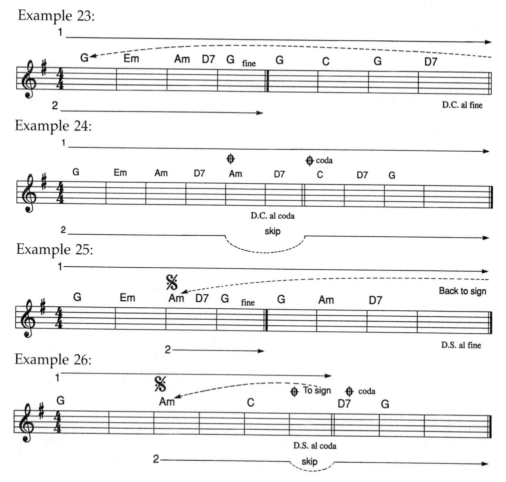

What Are Charts?

Now that we have gone over most of the symbols and words you will use and see in music notation, let's turn our attention to what actual charts in a recording or rehearsal situation look like. Instruments such as saxophone which play single-note lines read music in a very straightforward manner: the notes they are to play are simply written down.

Instruments which have to play chords as well as single notes have to have that chordal information conveyed in the chart as well as the notes. Guitar and bass parts using chord symbols are written identically, except that the guitar part uses the treble clef and the bass part uses the bass clef. The musical charts for bass and guitar (and often keyboards as well) usually consist of chord symbols as well as some rhythmic notation—in the form of actual notes or angular slashes demarking the beat. Whether or not the notes one wishes the player to play are specifically written out, the chord symbol should always appear above the staff (see letter A above).

Generally, guitar, bass, and keyboard parts are all very sparse in format; they leave much to the imagination and instinct of the musician. Regarding writing out very complicated parts, noted arranger, composer and educator Don Sebesky says:

> In an arrangement, I would almost never write out. . .an intricate. . .line because an inventive. . . player will create a better. . .line than I could ever write. I usually just indicate the chord symbols and leave it to the individual. . .player's musicianship and judgement to improvise a line accordingly.

This concept makes particular sense when working within a rock setting for any number of reasons. First, making an arrangement for a song with one's own band is often a cooperative process. Rarely does one player tell everyone else exactly what to do, as one finds in the case of the professional arranger. The mutual band effort necessarily calls upon the innate talents of all the musicians involved.

Second, the egos and self-perceptions of younger rock musicians are usually more tied to their creativity than those of hired studio players and seasoned musical veterans. Thus, there may be an element of diplomacy required in directing band players to play a specific part rather than fulfilling a specific role.

Third, there is always the consideration that a fairly complicated part, when written out, may be too difficult for the neophyte music reader to negotiate successfully. It's interesting to note here than many unschooled yet gifted instrumentalists can improvise a very complex musical line or rhythm but cannot read the same notes or rhythm when they are written out in standard music notation.

So, it's wise to know your musicians as well as you can in terms of their creativity, reading skills, and personality.

In a perfect world, all composers and arrangers as well as all other musicians would use the exact same chord symbols to identify various chords. In an imperfect world, one can expect to find variations in chord symbols from person to person and chart to chart. Throughout this book, we will write out chord symbols like these here:

Example 27:

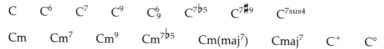

$C \quad C^6 \quad C^7 \quad C^9 \quad C^6_9 \quad C^{7\flat5} \quad C^{7\sharp9} \quad C^{7sus4}$

$Cm \quad Cm^7 \quad Cm^9 \quad Cm^{7\flat5} \quad Cm(maj^7) \quad Cmaj^7 \quad C^+ \quad C^\circ$

The word "minor" will be abbreviated "m," as in "Gm" (not "G minor" or "G min"). The word "major" will be written "maj," and the European "7" (the kind with a slash through it) will never be used. The shorthand notation for a flat or minor chord, "-" (the minus sign), which is often used in jazz charts, will never be used. A diminished chord will be expressed using the symbol "°" and augmented chords will be written using the "+" sign. A half-diminished chord will be written Cm7♭5, not C⌀. Below are a few measures from a chart which could be presented to a rhythm section consisting of bass, drums and guitar:

Example 28:

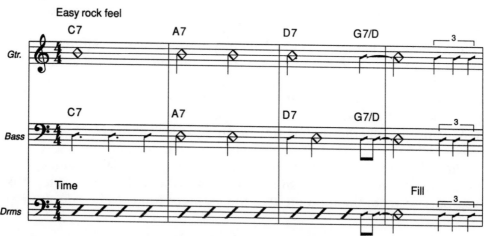

When chords are to be played in a whole note, half note, dotted half note or any particular rhythm, diamond-shaped symbols are used. The A7 chord in the fourth measure is to be played in a triplet rhythm. Triplets are three notes played in the space of two notes of the same duration.

The chord G7/D refers to a G7 chord with a D note in the bass. When a chord is to be played with a different note in the bass other than the root (name) of the chord, the bass note is placed below an oblique line.

In the third measure of the example above, the bassist is playing what is known as a syncopated rhythm. Syncopation means shifting the accent by playing on an unaccented beat, or on the last half of a beat. That is exactly what is happening here. The bassist is not playing on the (normally) accented first beat of the fourth measure; rather, the note is played on the "and-of-four"—the second half of the fourth beat of the measure. Syncopation is common to all forms of popular music, from rock to jazz, techno-pop to R&B.

Suppose the arranger wants to further accentuate this "off-beat"—from which comes our common word "offbeat"—by making the guitarist aware of the syncopation and enlisting his or her cooperation. The arranger then simply notates the same rhythm on the guitarist's chart:

Example 29:

Now the guitarist will play the G7/D chord using the rhythm notated in the arrangement. The bass and guitar will sound "tight," "locked in," or "together" in time when both musicians play the syncopated figure.

Before we bring the drummer into the arrangement, here is a quick but important thing to remember regarding guitar solos (or bass solos, for that matter) and chord notation. If there is to be a guitar or bass solo in the music, it's best to indicate it by writing the words "solo ad lib" ("ad lib" derived from the Latin "ad libitum" meaning at will) at the place where the solo is to begin and "end of solo" where the solo ends.

With regards to chord notation, when the guitar is to play a definite melodic line over a chord or a chord with a specific high or top note, it is necessary to write the top note that the arranger wants to hear as the top note in the chord. The guitarist must be trusted to play an appropriate voicing or formation of the chord.

We can illustrate this point by "dictating" the way we might want the guitarist in the previous example to play the four different chords. The notation "top" is sometimes added as a reminder.

Example 30:

There can be no doubt here that the arranger wants to hear an C7 chord with an C note as the top (highest) note and that this chord is to played in the rhythm specified by the chart.

Drum charts use various lines of the staff to represent the different elements of the basic drum or "trap" kit: bass drum, snare drum, tom-toms, cymbals, and hi-hats. Hi-hats are also cymbals, but they are really very different; hi-hats are actually two cymbals connected vertically through their centers with a rod which is attached to a foot pedal. By stepping on the foot pedal, the drummer can open or close the two cymbals. The hi-hat cymbals can be either fully or partially closed by means of a foot pedal. The classic "daah, di-di-daa" of swing is a hi–hat effect. Used in an appropriate way, the hi-hat is a terrific rhythmic tool.

While most cymbals have no definite pitch, drums can be and often are "tuned" to various pitches. A drummer will often tune his or her drums to pitches in a scale, for example. A drum fill or solo on a drum kit tuned this way adds an extra element of melody to the music which can be clearly heard as the drummer moves from one drum to another. Here's an example of how the lines of the staff can be used to specify certain drums:

Example 31:

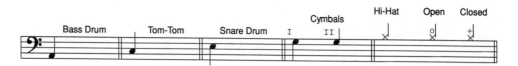

However, the drum chart for the four measure example written out above does not use this notation! The first difference is that this chart does not use the bass clef. Instead, a "clef" of no definite pitch is used here. The clef sign used above is the most common clef for indeterminate pitch.

Also, we see here that all that is notated is the instruction "time," the rhythmic figure which the bass is playing in the third measure and the cue for a drum fill on the last two beats of the fourth measure. When a drummer sees the notation "time," the arranger/composer is leaving the interpretation of the rhythm solely up to the drummer.

Almost all modern drummers play on a drumset which includes at least two tom-toms of varying pitch. To hear the acknowledged master of multiple tom-tom fills, listen to Hal Blaine's recordings. You've probably heard his exciting tom-tom technique on the theme song to television's *Hawaii Five-O* and you may be familiar with his fills on many early rock hits like the Ronettes' "Be My Baby." When one wants a drummer to play or two or more tom-toms or cymbals in a certain order, the chart will reflect this by using extra spaces as is done here:

Example 32:

Before ending this section on drum charts, there are two other things to bear in mind about writing drum charts. If a drum part seems to be running longer than two pages, the chart preparer should try to condense the chart wherever possible by using repeat signs, as below:

Example 33:

Note that the number of the measure should be notated on top of the staff to make it easier for the drummer to maintain his or her place in the music.

The second point is this: When a drum part is written out using all the various elements of the drum set, the notation can become cumbersome and confusing, especially if the part is supposed to be sight-read and played perfectly at first attempt.

It is always a good idea for the arranger to write the simplest drum part possible which can convey all of the important musical information. An example of this is the drum part in the scored chart for "Save The Last One For Me" at the beginning of this chapter (see page 34). This chart tells the drummer to play the hi-hat cymbals on every eighth note throughout the song. If the snare drum rhythm is not specifically notated, the drummer will instinctively play the snare on beats 2 and 4 of each measure (the backbeats) after spotting the word "rock" ("Heavy rock feel") at the top. It is important to notate the specific bassdrum pattern in this case, since it follows a distinctive rhythm.

Finally, if there is a chart for the keyboard player, it should outline both the chordal structure of the tune as well as the bass line. If only chord symbols are used, without specific instructions as to how the chords should be voiced, the bass line should still be included so that the keyboardist's own bass part—what the left hand plays—will not interfere or clash with the line being played by the bassist.

The chord symbols are often notated in between the two staffs, making the part easier to read by, in a sense, connecting the two staffs visually. Here's an example of such a part, which includes the rhythm of the bass part:

Example 34:

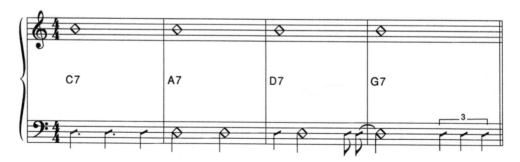

If the bassist will be playing a solo part or a very syncopated fill, it is often best to instruct the keyboardist to "lay out" or not play any bass notes at all in these places. This minimal concept in notation can best be described as "comping," which comes from the word "accompanying." Because the player is improvising both the voicings and rhythms, comping adds a great deal to the music in terms of the spontaneity by placing few restrictions on the musician.

In general, then, the keyboard or piano part will at least be comprised of the chord changes and the bass part of the piece, along with indications above the staff as to the style of playing desired.

There are, then, different levels of complexity that may be found in an arrangement. Part of this depends most times on how much the arranger decides to set out the parts for both the rhythm section and the soloists, but the complexity of an arrangement may also be the result of the input from the various members of the group. While the above example is acceptable under most circumstances, an easier way to convey the same information is simply to prepare one chart for the entire rhythm section. Once again, the arranger must be aware of the musicians' capabilities regarding their capacity to play the piece convincingly after only a brief run-through, if not upon first sight.

This "master chart" concept is really just the two staffs of music making up the keyboard chart. The bass player will read the bass part in the bass clef; the keyboard part is clear, while the electric lead will most probably play high-note accents on the second and fourth beats. The drummer will play whatever he or she usually plays for the particular feel.

One last point: Don't let the fear of having the musicians spontaneously create parts give rise to your own insecurities and drive you to write every single note and rhythm. Consistently stifling musicians' creativity like this could nominate you for a place on their list of least favorite arrangers.

It all seems rather complicated at first—there are so many things to remember—but there is a certain logic to the musical score once you get into it. Music, above all else, is systematic, and nowhere is this more evident than in the score. Once you get the hang of recognizing the time signature, for example, you will know that every measure is some many beats long—unless you get into some highfalooting modern piece where time signatures change left and right (or even some standards like the Beatles' "All You Need Is Love," which alternates measures of 4/4 and 3/4). And once you know what the clefs do, you will be able to spot the line on the staff that denotes the G or the F pitch without having to count lines and spaces.

What's more important, though, is that as you begin to see the logic of the score, you will also begin to see how logical music itself is. You will start seeing that certain chords just seem to go together. If you're doing a song in G, for example, somewhere along the line you're going to run into a D7 chord, and that D7 chord is most likely going to bring you back to G. You will see that the faster a song goes in terms of tempo, the more likely it is that the melody is not going to have a lot of different pitches in it. On slow songs, though, like a ballad, the melody is probably going to have a lot of what they call "contour"—where it goes up and down a fair amount.

There are all kinds of theoretical reasons for this, but they are not important for our purposes here. The thing is to start thinking about what makes you like the way in which a song is performed. When you're listening to a record, try to pick out the different instruments. What's the drummer doing? How many guitar tracks are there? How many vocals? What catches your ear? Is it the way the bassist seems to push the song forward or is it the rhythm of the riff and the way it plays against the basic beat of the song?

Just as important as understanding what you like about a performance is understanding what you don't like about one. The keyboards drown out the basic rhythm of the piece, or the bassist seems to be playing every note but the right one. Or you just can't get into the groove of the song.

Looking at a score allows you to see all the different ingredients that go into a musical performance. What you want to do is to be able to hear in your head how all the instruments go together and somehow get that across to your musicians. You can tell them, as Fruithead does, or you can learn to write it down.

But for all the different elements that go into an arrangement and all the different things you have to take into account as you begin arranging, there's one basic rule you should always bear in mind: keep it simple. Drummers only have two hands and two feet—that's as true for the legendary Steve Gadd as it is for Animal on *The Muppet Show*. Perhaps the most common problem in all arranging has to do with what happens at the low end. Bass players should not play as if they were frustrated lead guitarists; they are first and foremost essential parts of the rhythm section, helping not only to spot the harmony but drive the song along. The trouble comes when they try to do too much, cluttering up the rhythm and harmony. That's when these frustrated lead guitarists end up being just frustrating bass players.

You get the point, but there is another, even better reason for keeping it simple. As we will see in quotes from all the great arrangers, simple arrangements tend to bring out the best creativity, the spontaneity of all the musicians involved. So, start from the bottom and work up: get the rhythm right, and the rest will naturally follow.

3

How Arrangements Can Change a Song

In looking at scores and charts, we've already had a glimpse at the various elements that go into the arrangement—matters of rhythm (note values), harmony (chord notations and positions), form (the various repetition markings in their ways describe form), and, of course, orchestration. Charts and scores may be nothing but a collection of hen scratches and fly specks, but they certainly do provide an excellent introduction to the many different things the arranger has to think about.

But these are just some of the ingredients in the arrangement. Any cook can have a cupboard full of spices: the question is which spices go with which dish? In other words, what makes a good arrangement, well, good? And, for that matter, what makes a bad arrangement bad?

It has a lot to do with taste and exposure and experience. Recognizing a good arrangement is primarily an intuitive response. It conveys the feeling of the song; with good arrangements, you can sense what the song is about even if you can't hear the lyrics. A good arrangement will draw you into the song and make you want to experience it just once more time.

We aren't talking about the mix here—the mix is just the finishing touch on an arrangement that has already been recorded. We are talking about the groove of the rhythm, the combination of the instruments, the make-up of the vocals. We're talking about standing in a coffee shop and hearing a song you don't know and walking out of the place whistling it between your teeth, pacing your steps to its beat.

Okay. That's what a good arrangement does, but still there's the question of what is a good arrangement. Don Sebesky speaks of four things that are essential to good arranging: *balance, economy, focus,* and *variety.*

While these represent four different ideas musically, they are nonetheless interrelated, each exerting some influence on the others. Let's examine what he means by each of these, and then look at how each pertains to what we know about arranging.

Balance

When Sebesky speaks of "balance," he is referring to a number of things. First, he is talking about the balance between the tones of the various instruments (otherwise known as "timbre"). Then there is the balance between the instruments themselves (as they are spread across the registers from high to low). But as he is using it here, balance means more than just sound; it also refers to the interplay between the various melodic and harmonic ideas in the song.

The balance in instrumental timbre is often a matter of combining reedy or abrasive sounds with those that are softer, rounder. For example, in vocal arrangements, background vocals often work with "ooh" and "aah" sounds while the lead vocal tends to be tighter sounding, with a bit of an edge to it.

The balance in register is very much dependent on the style of the times. Whereas in the sixties, for example, producers like George Martin sought to cover the instrumental range from bass to treble fairly evenly, the shift in the seventies and eighties has been to a split between bass and treble, with less emphasis in the mid-ranges—consider, for example, the Police, who generally use a bass, guitar, and drums. In the Police, Andy Summers' effects on the guitar tended to place the instrument in the high range, particularly when he used boxes that enhanced the more aggressive, trebly timbres. With the bass and drums filling the bottom, this created an envelope to enclose Sting's vocals.

The last aspect of balance in the arrangement involves the time restrictions of the piece, the weight, if you will, of the component parts—the intro, verse, chorus, and so on. In this book, we will only be talking about arrangements for popular songs of a "recordable" length, about three minutes —the average length of the popular song since the inception of the 78 rpm recording.

The length of the piece is certainly a consideration in arranging. For example, a three-minute song should have an introduction, probably two verses, a chorus, perhaps an instrumental solo section and an ending. All of the instruments chosen to perform the piece must be introduced in some way during that time. With a longer piece, the arranger has, in a sense, more freedom to "stretch out" and develop the elements of the arrangement. This can often be more difficult than in the shorter piece, as the arranger is faced with more possibilities from which to choose.

Looking more closely, we can see that creating the balance between timbre and register of the instruments, important aspects of skillful orchestration, may be heard on such Beatle songs as "Yesterday" and "In My Life." The approach followed by George Martin in "Yesterday" was to have the song open with vocal and acoustic guitar before bringing in a string quartet (itself quite an innovation over the wash of strings typically used in the pop music of the time). In "In My Life," the song opens with a very airy electric guitar line set over a light rhythm accompaniment. The climax of the arrangement is the baroque-sounding piano solo in the instrumental section —the result of another Martin innovation, the use of half-speed recording (that is, recording a part slowly at half-speed and playing it back at normal) to achieve note-for-note clarity and precise rhythmic articulation.

The important thing to understand here is that an arrangement—any arrangement—should not have too many things going on at the same time, unless the specific goal is to create a frenzied sound. This kind of "over-arranged" arrangement might be called for in a song which expresses an hallucinogenic, angry, psychotic, or dissonant mood. In the main, though, it behooves the arranger to stay clear of including too much of anything— too many different melodies, too many different rhythms, too many instruments, too many fast notes.

Economy

Sebesky's idea of economy, as you can see, follows nicely from his sense of balance. In the matter of arranging, economy simply meaning omitting anything from the arrangement which is not absolutely necessary. Witness the string quartet as opposed to the string orchestra in "Yesterday," for example.

The Beatles' album *Abbey Road* is an excellent example of how two very different arranging concepts can be applied to the same band or group of musicians. The first side of the album opens with Lennon's rough and ready "Come Together" and includes such cuts as Harrison's ballad "Something," the fifties-sounding "Oh! Darling," and Starr's "Octopus's Garden," with its overall country rock feel. All of these songs have a definite beginning, exposition, and conclusion. They each sound different; they are each arranged without particular regard for one another. On the second side, however, all of the songs—especially "You Never Give Me Your Money," "Sun King," "Mean Mr. Mustard," "Polythene Pam," and "She Came In Through The Bathroom Window"—run together seamlessly as each song seems to be but a single movement of an larger work.

Producer/arranger George Martin comments about the music on the two sides of Abbey Road being as different from one another as the personalities of John Lennon and Paul McCartney:

I never thought we would get back together again. . . I said. . .if I have to go back and accept a lot of instructions I don't like, I won't do it. . .[*Abbey Road*] became a compromise, with one side of the album very much the way John wanted things—"Let it all hang out, let's rock a little"—and the other being what Paul had accepted from me: to try to think in symphonic terms, and think in terms of having a first and second subject, put them in different keys, bring back themes and even have some contrapuntal work. Paul dug that, and that's why the second side sounds as it does.

True, much of the genius of *Abbey Road's* second side must be attributed to Paul McCartney's songwriting, yet it works as a musical experience because of the arrangements. This brings together such a wide variety of material—Lennon's "Polythene Pam" is miles away from "You Never Give Me Your Money" or "Golden Slumbers"—and provides the material with focus, and yet it also maintains the integrity of the individual songs.

Focus and Variety

Economy, in Sebesky's use of the word, includes both focus and variety (as well as balance). We can interpret these terms as they relate to the arrangement of the second side of *Abbey Road.*

"Focus" means that there should always be one element of the music standing out during any particular time in the piece— something that can only be achieved if the arrangement is not too cluttered or busy. In "Golden Slumbers," for example, the piece opens with a solo piano playing simple chords for a few beats, then a solo voice enters singing the melody. After a few beats of melody ("*Once there was a way. . .*"), strings enter, followed by a single, extended bass note, which ties in with the closer to the opening line ("*to get back homeward*").

Thus, the groundwork for the first verse is set. The sparseness of the arrangement—a terrific demonstration of how a full string orchestra can be used sparsely—implies that there is more to come. Indeed, all this serves as preparation for the entry of the drums and guitars that accompany the vocalist for the second verse.

At various times during the first section of the song the primary focus has gone from the piano to the vocalist to the string section, and then the bass and the drums. All of these, when they are not the primary focus, are relegated to lesser but nonetheless important places of interest in terms of the arrangement.

The concept of "variety" refers to the arranger keeping the listener's interest by using different instrumental sounds and varying the tone color (timbre) of the music. When the focus changes, the tonal quality usually changes as well, but think of an example in which it doesn't: a piano duet which features one pianist and then the other. The sound is the same, but the music is not. When the timbre changes (think of a featured violin section and then a featured harp section), the focus usually changes as well. Of course, there are exceptions here as well: a vocalist being accompanied by first a guitarist and then by a keyboardist will still be the primary focus though the color will shift with the instruments.

Most of this book will be concerned with arranging for the small rock band, and therefore the variety of tone colors with which the arranger has to work will be less than those used by an arranger with access to a fuller range of instruments. Still, think of all of the variety of sounds which cover the "rock" spectrum, from a mellow country band with fiddle and steel guitar to a Frank Zappa-type group complete with a full horn section, percussionist(s), two or three guitars, and backup vocalists.

The broader area of rock certainly contains enough potential variety of its own to allow us to use the small combo setting as a subject for teaching some basic applications of arrangement. Though we have been speaking almost exclusively of original material up to this point, arranging can also be the means by which to rework an original. Let's look at a few songs which have been re-recorded ("covered") with an arrangement different from that used in the original version.

Two examples come to mind: the song "Jump," originally recorded by Van Halen and later covered by Aztec Camera, and "Viva Las Vegas," originally recorded by Elvis Presley and covered by the Dead Kennedys. The one thing that all four versions have in common is that they all belong to the same genre or type of music: rock. A further distinction can be made, citing that Van Halen's arrangement is "heavy metal," Aztec Camera's borders on "folk rock," Elvis's version is a "big-band rock/Vegas showtune" arrangement and the DK's sound is definitely "punk" or "thrash" rock.

Jump

A particular song can be arranged and covered in such as way as to move it from one genre to another, and we'll be talking about examples of this kind of "cross-genre" adaptation as well. Now, on to the two arrangements of "Jump" by Van Halen and Aztec Camera. Although the group Van Halen probably does not need much introduction, they are a California-based hard rock (some may say heavy metal) band comprised of electric guitar, electric

Example 35:

bass, amplified drums, and vocalist. Multi-track technology in the recording studio actually affects how many "band members" can appear in a recording. A single guitarist or keyboard player may play on three or four different tracks. It sounds like six musicians, but there are only two players. The only limit is the number of tracks available in the studio—usually sixteen or twenty-four.

We'll now examine portions of the original "Jump" recording, starting from the top. The song opens with a huge synthesizer sound; the chord is deep (low, bassy) and powerful, and forms the understructure for the entering chordal synthesizer line, played in a higher voicing by a "second synthesizer/person/track." After four measures, we hear some bass and drum accents as well as some primal vocal yells. After four more measures of the synth line, there's another bass and drum fill and then the rhythm or groove of the song commences. This continues for eight measures, the same synth part continuing throughout the first four and then changing slightly to something new yet connected during the last four bars. Then the vocalist enters singing the lyric to the tune and we are underway. If a score had existed for a record like this one, it might look like Example 35 on the previous page.

Now let's look at some of the parts notated above to see what effect they create in the arrangement. The tempo marking (mm= 134) denotes a moderate to fast pace. The notation "mf" (*mezzoforte*, "half loud") tells us that this song is to be played fairly loudly. Dynamics are a fairly relative thing —let's face it, a rocker's version of loud is quite different from that subscribed to by a classical player. In the recording studio, the actual volume of the various parts is controlled by the prominence of their corresponding tracks in the "mix," or relative volumes of each track in the final product.* The dynamic marking does, however, have some meaning to the musicians: it gives them a direction, in the sense that they may be playing forcefully with a "big" sound on their instruments. Some players play loudly in the studio; some do not. In either case, they are aware of how their sound is captured on tape and can thus adjust their playing according to how the producer/arranger wants to hear their part being performed. For instance, an engineer may mike a guitarist's amplifier to get that special sound that an electric can make only when it is on the verge of feedback. The guitar, then, will be played quite loudly. But the producer may want that particular

---

*The author wishes that the word "product" were not used when talking about musical pieces, but since the word has become part of the common parlance in the music industry, it's probably for the best that the reader appreciate this aspect of the bizspeak as well.

sound "back in the mix"—that is, he might want that tearing whine in the background, as part of the texture of the recording. So a live loud sound can be be made quiet on tape simply by twisting a knob.

We have spoken about a consistent eighth-note pattern on bass or guitar as a means of propelling the music. The constant rhythm of a jackhammer tearing up street pavement gives you a pretty good idea of what we mean by driving or pushing the music along. In Van Halen's "Jump," the bass player is a bit like a jackhammer, his driving rhythm united with the drummer's strokes—the classic rock drumbeat: eighth-notes on a cymbal and snare drum hits on 2 and 4.

The bass drum is not prominent in the mix but it seems as if he is playing the fairly typical rock rhythm notated above. There does not appear to be any guitar part during the verse, as the synthesizer provides all of the rhythmic and harmonic accompaniment. The synthesizer repeats the part it played on the introduction, which we see is very syncopated and thus adds an interesting counter-rhythmic element to the driving bass and drums.

Thus, every quarter and eighth note is accounted for by the rhythm section here. The Van Halen arrangement can be characterized as providing an overall propelling rhythm plus an interesting, bouncy keyboard part. When the vocalist enters, the primary focus shifts to him from the synth part.

Let's now compare the Van Halen arrangement up to this point with Aztec Camera's version of the song and see how they adapted "Jump" to their own sound and style. The first thing we notice is the tempo of this new version of "Jump," the metronome marking here being mm=120, which is a leisurely tempo as compared to the slightly faster (though still moderate) marking of mm=134 for Van Halen's rendition.

But the biggest difference is heard immediately: Aztec Camera's record opens up with an acoustic guitar playing the core of the line performed in the Van Halen version by the synth player, but in a more fluid (less staccato) way. The guitarist is accompanied by a very sparse bass and drums and what sounds like another acoustic guitar playing very simple fills, an example of which is included below. Already, the feel of the song is so overwhelmingly dissimilar that it sounds like another tune! If there were a score for a performance like this, it might be written as in Example 36 on the next page.

Example 36:

This mellow intro provide an appropriate setting for the vocal entrance, which sounds lethargic, almost comical, when singing the first words "I get up." At this point, the bass and drums vary their parts slightly. The drum now plays the basic rock eighth-note cymbal rhythm and 2 and 4 accents on the snare (the tambourine follows the snare beat) while the bass plays a slightly more "notey" line.

Even with these changes, the feel remains constant. The groove of the rhythm section is still very light and airy even as it becomes more active.

Let's try to imagine what kind of things Aztec Camera were thinking about when they decided to cover "Jump." First of all, there is the choice of this particular song. Clearly, band members liked the song, its compositional and lyrical interest. And then there is the undeniable fact that the song had been a tremendous success when it first appeared. We really don't know exactly why Aztec Camera picked this particular song to cover but let's assume that they were aware of the fact that "Jump" did well for Van Halen on the charts (the *Billboard* "Top 40" or "Hot 100" listings of record sales, not the "charts" we refer to when talking about writing out music), and they felt that they could adapt it to their own unique sound and style.

The task of the arranger in this instance is to take a song written in one style and, by working with a new instrumentation, alter the basic feel or mood of the tune. Specifically, the arranger must address the challenge of turning a hard rock/heavy metal song into a light-rock song to be recorded by a band espousing an eclectic style.

We'll now see how this idea came to fruition. After abandoning the heavily electrified instrumentation of Van Halen, the song was re-orchestrated. We have seen that the synthesizer part was given to an acoustic guitar. This change alone would be enough to move the song from the realm of hard rock into the area of light-rock or, one might even say, folk-rock. How about the use of the rhythm section in the opening? Van Halen's intro builds by having the bass and drums play simple, forceful parts, climaxing with an outrageous scream that leads directly into the body of the song. Aztec Camera starts the groove going immediately, and later makes it just a bit more driving. There are no huge crashes, no big chords, no heavy drum accents or fills to speak of in their version. The basic sound of the arrangement has already been defined by the acoustic guitar, easy-sounding ("laid back") drum part and simple bass part. One instrument—a percussion instrument —has been added to the rock rhythm section and that is a tambourine, a callback to the kinder, gentler sounds of 60s rock and folk-rock.

Just as the instrumentation varies, so do the vocals. Though they differ greatly from one another, they manage to bring out a distinctive aspect of the lyric. Notice that both versions are in the key of C major. David Lee Roth, Van Halen's vocalist, sings right at the listener, full voice, in a very direct and aggressive style. You can almost see him throwing out each word as if it were a projectile hurtling through space.

Aztec Camera's vocalist, on the other hand, sings in a style which could be described as relaxed, unselfconscious, indifferent, unanimated. This is not a negative comment on his singing, but rather, a reflection of the mood they have created in the instrumental arrangement. But boy, do the two vocals sound so amazingly different!

How can this be? Both songs are in the same key, but Aztec Camera's vocalist is singing the melody an octave (twelve half steps, from C to C) lower than David Lee Roth. By itself, regardless of singing style, this does much to change the frenetic Van Halen vocal into something more sedate. So we see that even though the key has remained the same from one version to the next, the range, the register in which the vocal is sung has a great effect upon the sound of a piece of music, and can be varied to achieve various ends.*

Altering the structure or form of a song will have an effect on the overall sound of an arrangement. Van Halen's version runs about 3' 50'' while Aztec Camera's lasts for a little over five minutes. Given the drastic change in the length of the song, it seems pretty clear that the arranger wanted to say something through the addition of so much time.

Four minutes is about the maximum length that a single record should last if one wants to get airplay on most radio stations, and it is fair to say that one hears more short hit songs on radio than long ones. There are exceptions, however, and one of the more notable exceptions to the "three minute rule" is Queen's "Bohemian Rhapsody." Only a handful of songs longer than three or four minutes have been successful in terms of airplay; Bob Dylan's "Rainy Day Women Numbers 12 and 35," Richard Harris' "MacArthur Park," and the Beatles' "Hey Jude" are the few examples that come to mind.

Queen's record company balked at releasing the seven-minute "Bohemian Rhapsody" but the song was released after its pre-release airplay received a tremendous reception from the listening public. The tune went on to become the number one record for six weeks in England as well as making the top ten in America. Not too shabby for a seven-minute single with an opera section!

---

*Another case in point is W. Axl Rose from Guns 'N' Roses. With that terrific range of his, he often begins a song in one register that moves higher as the song progresses to increase the tension of the mood, as in "Sweet Child O' Mine."

Length, though, generally does affect commercial viability of a pop song. We'll talk about what that meant in terms of these two versions of "Jump" later on. First, let's take a look at the outlines of the structures of both arrangements of the song.

Van Halen	Aztec Camera
Intro	Intro
Verse 1	Verse 1
Chorus	Chorus
Verse 2	Verse 2
Chorus	Chorus
Solo section: guitar	Chorus
then synthesizer	Guitar solo until end
Intro	
Chorus, repeat and fadeout	

All other considerations aside, both songs proceed in the same manner through the second chorus.

There the similarity ends. Van Halen modulates (changes) keys for a trademark heavy metal guitar solo followed by a synthesizer solo. After this musical highpoint in the arrangement, the opening is re-stated and followed by a repeating chorus which is faded out (gradually reduced in volume by the recording engineer) until the end. Aztec Camera's arrangement changes dramatically after the last chorus in its version; a crescendo lasting 16 measures leads up to a freeform Hendrix-like guitar solo complete with feedback, which accounts for over a third of the song's entire length!

Now let's return to the concept of a "commercial arrangement" for a moment. Radio and video airplay, the arbiters of commerciality in modern pop music, seem to favor those songs which follow predictable patterns in their structure. It may be said of the orderly procession of verse and chorus that this format is more easily grasped and remembered by the listener than more imaginative arrangements. Whatever the case may be, both arrangements of "Jump" are imaginative in their respective ways. The Van Halen one uses a keyboard where one would expect to hear Eddie Van Halen's signature guitar and there is a fairly infrequent modulation from the key of C major to B minor for the guitar solo. The song returns to C major for the synth solo and stays in that key throughout the remainder of the song.

None of these things prevented the song from being a big hit as the song still followed a fairly straightforward single format.

Aztec Camera's version, on the other hand, has the words "album cut" written all over it. The adaptation of a hard rock song into an eclectic rock song of mixed influences requires a certain courage as well as creativity and imagination. While there might be a tradeoff here in terms of artistic principle and commerciality, part of Aztec Camera's motivation might very well have been to take an icon of contemporary rock music—a very big hit—and have fun with it, rather like a bluegrass band doing a version of the reggae classic "The Harder They Come." But strictly speaking, it is pretty fair to say there is little commercial potential for a song which involves a one minute and 35 second guitar solo that doesn't even start until three minutes and 30 seconds into the song.

It's not that this arrangement does not feature many of the characteristics described by Don Sebesky above, but economy in the commercial realm is even more stringent than one would find in matters of simple good taste.

The point to be understood here is that both arrangements are good arrangements—in fact, they are both excellent arrangements. Each emerges from a different point of view; each establishes and meets its own particular goal. The result is that while they are of the same song, they work with different tools and end up creating entirely different performances.

Another point to be made here has to do with taking risks. We spoke of Aztec Camera being courageous in approaching "Jump" the way they did; it was also somewhat courageous on the part of their record company to let them do it. Generally, the more established the artist, the easier it is for that performer to deviate from the accepted norms of commerciality. But even established artists sometimes have to fight for what they want. David Bowie, who has always tried to make interesting records, is a good case in point. Though he had been a major star for almost a decade, his label did not want to release his 1977 recording *Low* because Bowie did not sing much on it. After much hemming and hawing, the label released the album, with the ironic twist that the first single, "Sound and Vision," did not feature any Bowie vocals until a minute and a half into the song.

But the proof is in the pudding: more than ten years after its recording, *Low* is widely regarded as a significant trendsetter in the recording industry. The lesson for you in all this is to believe in what you do, and it will eventually find its place.

Viva Las Vegas

Can two musical artists be imagined who are more dissimilar than Elvis Presley and the now-defunct Dead Kennedys? The latter were a San Francisco-based politically and socially oriented punk group led by lead singer Jello Biafra. Their original lyrics express an anarchist, left-wing philosophy and we should probably bear this in mind as we look at their cover version of Elvis' "Viva Las Vegas." Jello Biafra is satirizing the values espoused in "Viva Las Vegas," so the aim of the entire arrangement seems more to parody than pay tribute to the King. Elvis needs no introduction.

"Viva Las Vegas" is the title track from one of the many films Elvis did during the period when he wasn't giving personal appearances. To suit the frenetic pacing of the place and the events in the story, Elvis' rendition has a metronome marking at about 300. The Dead Kennedys, not to be out-done, play it even faster, about mm=320.

This is about as fast as you can play rock while still keeping the semblance of a groove. At such tempos, accents lose their prominence—every nuance tends to get flattened. There is not much difference between the keys of the two versions: Elvis sings the song in G major while Jello prefers the key of A major. The key of A major is a particularly good one for songs featuring rock guitar as the guitarist can play the guitar's open (unfretted or unstopped) strings, which are ringy and sustain nicely. Elvis' version lasts about 2:10 and the DK's lasts about 2:30; not too much difference here either. Furthermore, both versions open with a short intro and proceed in exactly the same manner through verse, chorus, bridge, verse, and chorus.

So how do the arrangements differ from one another? To answer to this question, let's look at the orchestration, basic rhythm (groove) and individual parts of Elvis' piece and the cover version. It's easier to discuss the Dead Kennedys' orchestration first, as the band consisted of a single guitarist (who recorded two separate rhythm and lead guitar tracks on this song), electric bassist, drummer, and solo lead vocalist.

This is the configuration of the basic rock power trio plus a singer, like the Who or U2. On this track, then, we hear two guitars, bass, drums, and a vocalist. They enter in a "stacked" manner, which means one instrument is added "on top of" the other, one by one. This gives the arrangement a sense of being "built up" in the same way that any building is constructed, brick by brick. What follows is one possible score for the introduction to a hardcore punk version of a song like *"Viva Las Vegas"*:

Example 37:

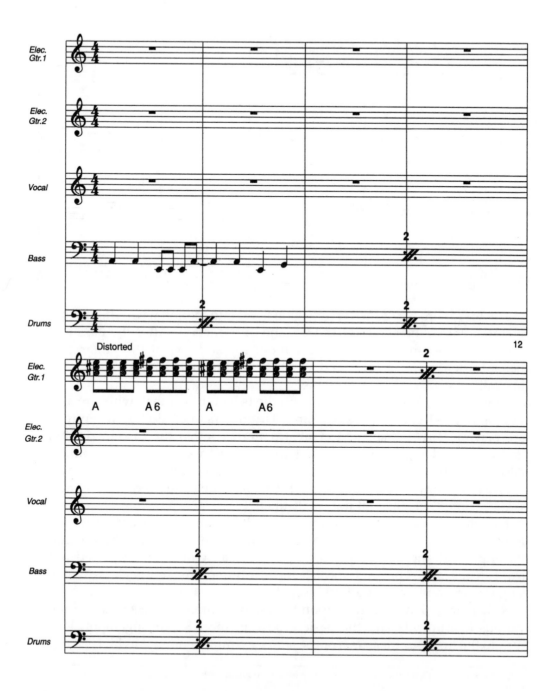

The feel or groove of the verse section is set into motion when the rhythm guitarist enters the song at bar 13 of the introduction. After the bass and drums have established the basic tempo, the addition of the guitar part helps to define the groove, and what we find is that this arrangement is basically a samba* in rock dressing!

Note that the drummer is playing on the bell of the cymbal, which results in a more precise, less splashy sound. Drummers often do this when they are playing fairly syncopated cymbal patterns—often the case in rhythm and blues and funk music (but not true in hard rock or metal or punk). Also, since the tempo here is really fast, any elaborate cymbal part will sound too "ringy" if played right on the large cymbal area because the individual "notes" or hits will not be distinctive.

The rhythm guitar sounds appropriately distorted and constant (the Ramones provide an excellent example of this steady, incessant rhythm guitar approach) and the simple high-pitched lead guitar line is placed out front in the mix. The lead vocal evinces a humorous approach, with the singer using a phoney southern accent.

Now that we have touched upon the instrumentation, the sounds of the various instruments and the basic groove in the DK's arrangement, let's turn to the first four measures of the above example rendered in Elvis' style:

---

*The samba is a Brazilian dance in 2/4 time which became popular in the United States in the late thirties.

Example 38:

*Col means "to follow along" so the piano plays along with the guitar and bass parts

The music really has a strong "two" feel, thanks, as always, to the bass and drums. The bassist is playing the duple samba rhythm. The drum part adds to this groove by playing a sixteenth-note pattern on the snare which is a variation on a rhythm called "swamp beat." Added to these two rhythm section parts is a woodblock, a percussion instrument associated with Latin rhythms, and a maracas or shaker. The percussion accents come on the same beats as the bass player's accents, so they enhance the samba groove.

This is an important concept for the neophyte arranger to understand: the rhythm groove comes about by the thoughtful selection of parts and purposes for the individual players, or by the thoughtful creation of parts by the musicians themselves. Every player, in the truest sense of the word, is doing his or her part to create the feel of the tune. The woodblock subtly adds to the rhythm by playing "along with" the bassist. The pianist's comping (chordal accompaniment) also follows the same samba rhythm.

There is no need for each instrument to play the exact same accented rhythm in order to express a groove or feel for a song. Indeed, as we saw with the Dead Kennedys, though the bass and drums establish the tempo, the groove doesn't happen until the rhythm guitar comes in. The various players add their particular components to make the groove happen. In the Elvis version, it is sufficient for the bass, piano, and woodblock to accent the same beats. The samba is a dance; the rhythm needs to be there, but it is a very light rhythm, set by the bass and the drums here and reinforced by less prominent instruments. The principles of economy and balance are certainly at work here.

How about the sounds of various instruments in Elvis' version? Do the bass, drums, and guitar sound as they do in the Dead Kennedys' cover of the tune? Not at all! The bass in Elvis' version actually sounds like an acoustic bass, which has a warmer, less sustainy, more "woody" sound than the electric bass. The drummer sounds like he's playing lightly, with brushes on the snare drum. There may even be an acoustic rhythm guitar on the record, although it's not easy to hear. James Burton's tone on the electric guitar, which plays the intro line and many country-like fills during the tune, is twangy and bright, not the least bit distorted or "heavy" sounding. The twangy guitar adds a country-rockabilly element to the basic samba-rock rhythm of the song. Most country and bluegrass music is also in duple meter, so the meshing of this style with a Latin groove also in duple meter works well, and gives this arrangement a unique sound.

In summary, then, the instruments used in both arrangements are not too dissimilar from one another, yet the manner in which they are played and recorded accounts for the the striking difference in the effects of each upon the listener. The strong 4/4 feel of the Dead Kennedys' version contrasted with the 2/4 feel of Elvis' version is the other major element which accounts for the difference in grooves. One groove is a "punk samba" and one is a "country samba." Both are valid expressions of a mood, and the principles of variety, focus, balance, and economy have been attended to in each arrangement.

In this section we have been looking at how the arrangement can totally change the sound and therefore the perception of a particular piece of music. In reference to Don Sebesky's four elements of good arranging—balance, economy, variety, and focus— we have seen how the success of the arrangement depends on everything from the choice of instrumentation and tempo to the sequence of the component parts of the song. Further, as we have seen, choices in one area—to achieve balance in instrumental timbre, for example—affect choices elsewhere—in the economical use of instrumentation. In that sense, arranging is a bit like a kitchen cabinet in a slapstick comedy—slam one door and another one pops open.

Nowhere is the importance of the arrangement more evident than in the discrepancies between different versions of the same song. In the hands of Van Halen, "Jump" is a classic piece of good-time semi-metal pop, but when Aztec Camera arranges the song to suit their style, what we hear is a completely different tune. "Viva Las Vegas" as performed by Elvis Presley is a happy-go- lucky uptempo song; in the hands of the Dead Kennedys, though, it becomes a sarcastic commentary on the very "hard-livin', good-lovin'" attitude that informs the Elvis recording.

So many songs have been re-arranged and re-recorded that it is impossible to list them all here, but here are just a few titles with which you may be familiar: "Walk This Way" (first done as a hard rock tune by Aerosmith and then later covered in the rap/hip-hop style by Run-DMC), "Hazy Shade Of Winter" (penned and recorded by Simon & Garfunkel and later covered by the Bangles), "Up On The Roof" (recorded by Carole King, the Drifters, James Taylor, and others), "Baby It's You" (recorded by the Shirelles, the Beatles, and Smith, among others), and "Please Mr. Postman" (first by the Marvelettes, then the Beatles, and lastly—and certainly leastly—the Carpenters).

Give them a listen and try to hear where they are similar and where they are different. The point to be understood here is that there are really very few "rights" or "wrongs" in the realm of arranging. But there are good arrangements and bad ones. The most important thing when first approaching a song is to be sure of what you are trying to say with it. If your "vision" of the song is clear, the arrangement may simply fall into your lap. True, that vision may change: John Lennon in his post-Beatle years claimed that they often did his songs too fast. But they still sound pretty good, don't they?

Another point to be made here is that if you aren't sure about how you want your song to sound—you think you want a string sound here, but then you want a calypso band sound to rip through the bridge after a hammered dulcimer has finished playing the solo—then you might be trying to say too much with too little. One of the toughest parts of arranging is making choices between good ideas that don't work with each other. Don't worry about it: there will always be other songs, your own or somebody else's, that will give you the room and the place to fulfill your vision.

Who Does the Arranging?

Remember Fruithead, that zany, madcap songwriter who penned the classic "Save The Last One for Me?" Earlier on it was noted that the fictitious Fruithead, with the help of the other band members, structured her song's form and provided the musical information (tempo, dynamics, etc.), and became the de facto arranger of the song "Save The Last One for Me." Among the thousands of practicing bands, reality most often mimics this scenario, and the larger concept of The Arranger is brought into play.

Today, in much of the recording and playing of live music, the traditional professional arranger is now only employed when specific horn, string, and occassionally rhythm section parts are required.

Larry Saltzman, musical director, conductor, arranger, and guitarist for a major international star, relates a story about a recording artist who did an album in collaboration with another eminent arranger. The music, Saltzman comments, sounded first-rate with the parts well-constructed and artistically performed. Knowing that this arranger was expressly brought into the project because of his particular style, he (Saltzman) expected that there would be actual musical parts given to the musicians and that there would be some degree of musical notation involved. The truth is that when the charts were distributed to the studio players, there was very little musical notation to be found. What was notated were the key, tempo, bass part, chord changes, and dynamics. The extraordinary parts were created by the musicians as improvisations ("instant compositions") over a series of chord changes.

So who did the "arranging," and what did the "arranger" do? Experience tells us that in this case, the hired arranger most probably served as much the function of the record producer as that of the arranger in the traditional sense of the word. There are so many situational variables in the recording studio that one should be familiar with the functions of the various personnel who operate in the musical environment: the arranger, producer, songwriter, and of course, the musician. We know about the elements of arranging and therefore the duties of an arranger. The musician's job, as well as to play music, may also encompass some of the traditional functions of the arranger, as was the case above. The songwriter often acts as arranger in that he or she will have a certain rhythm or part "in their head" and will then express it to the musicians, either by humming a part or referring to a hit song he or she may have heard.

But isn't this part of the production of the musical piece, and isn't this really a job for the producer? Yes and no.

Distinctions between the duties and, subsequently, the "titles" of musical personnel in the studio have lessened with the advent of rock music. This is because so many acts (bands, groups) are self-contained, meaning that the songwriting, playing, arranging, and often production duties are being handled by the members of the band themselves as well as by outside specialists. Some bands also do their own managing and booking, mostly at the more beginning levels of the music business. As regards the true role of the producer, most producers would agree that their main function is to lend an objective ear to the music.

Back in the fifties, the roles of those involved in the music creation process were much more specified than they tend to be today. "A & R men" (meaning Artists and Repertoire) worked for the various record companies, and they could be either musicians, arrangers, or conductors (today, these erstwhile A & R men are known as producers). The control booth of the recording studio was their private domain, and their primary purpose was to choose material ("repertoire") for their acts ("artists") to record. For the most part, songs were submitted by music publishers directly to the A & R men.

This process still goes on today, albeit to a much lesser extent because so many of the bands and performers are self-contained. The process back then followed a fairly fixed routine: material was selected for an artist, an arranger was hired to arrange the publisher's song to suit the artist's style, then the arranger would hire a musical contractor who in turn hired the musicians to record the tune. Jerry Leiber, noted songwriter, musician and producer comments:

> It was not a very organic process—production was not as closely knit, in terms of being involved with every step of the process, as. . . I finally got involved in.

With the incessant search for new sounds and constant aural excitement, there has developed much in common between the roles of the producer, engineer, and arranger. If the engineer records in such as way as to create a new sound, or if he or she creates a unique, unheard-of effect, then the engineer is contributing in a very specific way to the arrangement in the area of timbre or, in the greater sense, orchestration. It's as if another instrument/sound was added, without anyone having to play the instrument; the engineer in this case is the "player," as well as the arranger of the sound of the recording. No one would argue with the producer's right to bring in additional musicians to a session, and it should be understood how the engineer can influence the recording process by bringing in new sounds.

Richard Perry, who has produced records for Diana Ross, Ringo Starr, Tiny Tim, Barbra Streisand, and the Pointer Sisters (among many others), credits his successful career to being articulate and having good communication skills. Keith Forsey, musician and songwriter, who has moved into the production of records (Billy Idol, Psychedelic Furs, Donna Summer), puts it this way:

> I try to stay out of their [the musicians'] face. My job is to be the mirror.

Other noted producers have the following to say about producing records: Teo Macero (Miles Davis' longtime producer):

> The producer's role is to encourage the musician to do whatever he wants, and to help him.

Narada Michael Walden (Jeff Beck, Aretha Franklin):

> Being a producer's just being able to have a sense of balance.

In looking at what Walden has to say, one may argue that the sense of balance within a musical piece may reflect the balance of the arrangement. The producer may be responsible for this element as well as other elements which we have included as belonging to the area of arranging—but then again, so may the songwriter, so may the musicians. The arranger, then, for our purposes, should have an objective musical ear as well as the ability to communicate certain ideas to the musicians as well as to the engineer. The engineer, for his part, must know how to capture the sounds on tape that the arranger/producer/songwriter/musician hears in his or her head. We have seen how informal communication can serve this purpose in our fictitious example of the Pits, Fruithead's band. We have also seen how charts can express musical information in a more standardized way. Following are some comments on the communication and perception of musical ideas by drummer Mike Fink, who plays with Ron Wood of the Rolling Stones as well as with Bo Diddley, one of the best known of the early rhythm and blues rockers.

Fink explains that, from a drummer's unique point of view, we have now entered the era of the drum machine. He says that today, the producer/arranger/songwriter often comes to a recording session armed with a drum machine, plugs it in, presses "Play" and says "Here's the beat." The drummer may take over at this point and weave his or her particular magic over the basic drum track, either playing along with the drum machine or copying the exact rhythm playing "live."*

Fink further explains that a familiarity with current hit songs is necessary for the successful communication of ideas—rhythmic, melodic, and harmonic—to the players. The seasoned veteran may comprehend that instructions to play "boom-boom-boom, boom-chaka-boom" may mean that a Latin beat is desired, while "Give me more movement" is actually a request for sixteenth notes on the hi-hat (alternately verbalized as "shakka-shakka-shakka-shakka"), but saying "play the beat like the Police song on the radio" could save hours in trial and error experimentation. Most self-contained rock bands, before entering the recording studio, work out their individual parts in pre-production, which is the hours spent in rehearsal studios, basements, or garages. This pre-production usually follows the "try this, try that" approach which leads to "head arrangements" of the song. "Head arrangement" is a common term used by musicians which refers to an arrangement which is not written down but is notated "in the head" of the player.

Fink's experience drumming with Bo Diddley serves well here. Bo Diddley is a former boxer and product of the "chitlin circuit," a bawdy bluesman and elder statesman of rock with considerable style, presence, and historical significance. He is not musically sophisticated in the sense that he would not be expected to say "I want you to play a dotted sixteenth-note pattern on the third beat." Bo Diddley never personally rehearses and Fink assumed that his job as drummer was to play the "Bo Diddley beat" or "Tradesman's Knock." This beat was succcessfully incorporated into songs like "Not Fade Away" by the Rolling Stones and Buddy Holly, Duane Eddy's "Can-

---

*For more on MIDI, computers, and arranging, please see Part III.

nonball," and "Hey Little Girl" by Dee Clark. This is what the "Bo Diddley" beat looks like:

Example 39:

However, the bandleader told Fink, "*Don't* play the Bo Diddley beat. Play quarter notes on the bass drum, 2 and 4 on the snare and eighth notes on the hi-hat because Bo likes to play the beat."

After arriving at the television studios for a taping of the *Joan Rivers Show,* the band prepared for its first live rehearsal. Bo Diddley loved what Fink was doing, but Bo's manager wanted the Bo Diddley beat played the way it was played on the original recording. So Mike Fink then played the beat the way he had remembered hearing it on the record "Bo Diddley" (the first record on the Chess label by the artist Bo Diddley—things were a bit strange back in the early days of rock). Bo heard the beat and said "No, no, no; it's a musical phrase I want." He then proceeded to sing the musical phrase to his drummer: "Bokka-dooka-doom, b'doom-doom." As he sang this, he pointed to the various tom-toms on which the "notes" of the musical phrase were to be played. This effective bit of communication led to the following drumbeat:

Example 40:

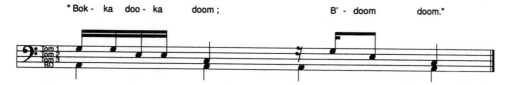

Who did the arranging? In this case, the drumbeat was "arranged" by the songwriter/artist, while all of the other band members fell in line accordingly with their self-created parts. All were based upon the basic seed of the arrangement, which was a groove or feel called the "Bo Diddley beat." The musical director or leader of the backup band attempted to "arrange" the drum part, but it wasn't what the manager wanted! The appropriate drumbeat came about as a result of direct communication between the musician and the songwriter.

Aretha Franklin is an example of a major recording star who relies heavily upon the impromptu arrangement for creating her music. It is well-known that her preferred way of working in the studio is to play a song alone on the piano, then have the rhythm section join in, instantly working out their accompaniment. At that point, the producer/arranger might switch some chords and figure out the final sequence of the various sections of the tune. Sometimes the horn players arrive later on to record their parts, which could be little more than a few notes jotted down on a sheet of paper!

Here is another anecdote which further illustrates the prevalence of impromptu arrangements in the recording field: Upon arriving at a London rock recording session, musically sophisticated producer/arranger from the States asked the record company executive in charge of the session if he could have a look at the musicians' parts. The musicians, as it happened, were first-rate American session players who were brought in specifically to get the "American" sound, whatever that was considered to be at the time. The producer was informed that there were no "parts," and that the players could just run through the song and make up their parts on the spot, as was the practice of the local English musicians when playing on rock records. He responded by jotting down some chords and outlining some drum fills and bass patterns just before the tape was about to roll.

One wonders if the music would have turned out any differently had the producer done nothing in terms of "arranging." It seems fair to say that this particular producer felt more comfortable having some written music rather than none at all. Perhaps knowing that there was something on paper to refer to, however basic it was, made the producer more relaxed and self-confident and thus more effective.

The popularity of head arrangements coupled with the demise of the traditional arranger (due to the appearance of self-contained bands in the mid-sixties) have had the combined effect of allowing virtually any and everyone involved in the music creation process to wear the hat of the arranger at one time or another. So, when we ask who does the arranging, we are not talking about an "arranger" *per se*. And when we talk about arrangers from now on, don't envision them as vague creatures armed with manuscript paper and pen, ready to add strings and horns to your latest hard rock composition. For the most part, YOU will be the arranger and it is with this in mind that we'll proceed through the various rock genres with an eye towards how musical arrangements vary from one style to another.

A good way to begin thinking about yourself as an arranger for your own material is to think of the contribution which George Martin made to the Beatles' music as a producer/arranger. He would first hear the music sung by the principal writer—either John Lennon or Paul McCartney—with a solo acoustic guitar or piano accompaniment. Then Martin would decide upon the "makeup" of the band: not too difficult a task, with two guitars, bass, and drums. Occasionally a keyboard would be added, usually played by Martin. The introduction, solo(s), song length and ending would be "arranged," and the task of "arranging" the tune would be done.

Most probably, arranging for your own group will follow many of these same parameters, assuming a minimal level of development in the songs that you are arranging. There's no need to get hung up on various titles or roles. What is most important in creating a musical expression is the final effect the music has upon the listener. Whether you actually "are" the songwriter, musician, producer, or arranger or are merely wearing that hat for the time being, it should have absolutely no effect on the professionalism you bring to your work.

PART II
Clothing the Beast

5

Arranging Rock Styles

Introduction

Rock music is the bastard child of blues and country music, its parents coming from different regions, different states, even different time zones. We can find its sources in places as far apart as Memphis, Austin, Kansas City, and Chicago.

Its direct lineage traces back to the rockabilly music of the 1950s. The music of such artists as Elvis Presley, Jerry Lee Lewis, Gene Vincent, and Carl Perkins typifies this "hillbilly rock" sound. Elvis is best known for commercializing the music of his rockabilly and rhythm and blues counterparts, drawing upon such varied influences as Hank Snow, Bill Monroe, and Arthur "Big Boy" Crudup. Elvis—the King of Rock—loved country music so much that "Blue Moon of Kentucky" was his first recording for the Sun label.

The term "rock 'n' roll" was coined to describe much by the likes of Chuck Berry and Buddy Holly, whose music featured crisp guitar licks and clever, imaginative lyrics. Since the early sixties, the era of the Beatles—who played, among other styles, rock 'n' roll and rockabilly—the term "rock" has been coupled with various adjectives to distinguish many different sub-genres including hard rock, light rock, heavy metal, hardcore punk/thrash rock, southern rock, new wave rock, Christian rock, and so on. Today, as a definition of a particular music style or genre, the word "rock" has become essentially meaningless. Furthermore, the truisms that the blues was a black person's music while rock was the domain of whites is no longer relevant—and thankfully so. Just witness the emergence of acts like Roachford, a black hard rock band complete with heavy metal guitar and Charley Pride, seminal black country singer. Not to mention Prince, whose songwriting and performing repertoire covers everything from Hendrix to John Lennon—he has even had a song on a recent "new folk" music sampler on Wyndham Hill Records!

Producer/Engineer Arthur Baker notes:

> Prince and all these other acts...are black but are doing rock 'n' roll,
> they just know they can relate to everybody.

On the other hand, people like George Thorogood and Eric Clapton play really convincing blues. Make no mistake, though: the blues, as we will see, is one of the great African-American contributions to popular music, if not the most noteworthy. But these and other "rock" musicians incorporate the scales, chords, and themes of the traditional blues. Think of the chords and melodies to songs like Cream's "Sunshine Of Your Love," Santana's "Black Magic Woman," Steppenwolf's "Born To Be Wild," The Kinks' "All Day And All Of The Night" and Smokey Robinson's "Get Ready." Look really closely and what you'll see in all of these songs is the predominance of the minor pentatonic scale. Here are parts of the melodies to songs like the ones listed above, all written in the same key, using the C minor pentatonic scale:

Example 41:

"Sunshine"

Example 42:

"Black Magic"

Example 43:

"Born Wild"

Example 44:

"All Day"

Example 45:

"Ready"

The closest any of these comes to being a pure "blues" as opposed to "rock" is "Black Magic," as its form and harmonies follow the twelve-bar structure we will be discussing in the next chapter. On the whole, though, one would not call any of the other songs "blues" songs. They are rock tunes, in no uncertain terms. So, what is rock? One definition which has been offered is that rock is any popular music with a simple, driving beat and a small-band instrumentation that features guitar and vocals. This definition might have been acceptable a few years ago, but the recent coming of age of the rap, hip-hop and "scratch" styles of music—not solely "black," it should be noted, with reference to rappers like the Beastie Boys—negates the part about featuring guitars. Guitars are often not present on many of the hi-tech productions today, and they were conspicuously absent on much of the keyboard-oriented "new wave" music of the early eighties by bands like the Human League and Kraftwerk.

Conversely, the mere addition of heavy sounding, distorted electric guitar (the "Marshall" sound, after the amplifier by the same name which yields the archetypal heavy guitar tone) does not automatically qualify a song as being heavy metal or hard rock. Megastar Madonna often incorporates the heavy guitar sound into her music, and various people will alternately describe her as being either a rock artist or a disco artist! Listen to "Like A Prayer" to hear distorted guitar used to great effect.

Next point: rock or disco? To discuss this point intelligently, we must first look at one idea which forever changed the face of the entertainment industry: the twelve-inch extended-play (EP) dance single, which surfaced in the late seventies. The effect which the twelve-inch dance single had upon the recording industry was to lump together many diverse genres into a new category called "dance music." This included records by artists like Talking Heads ("new wave"), Herbie Hancock ("jazz-rock" or "fusion") and Bruce Springsteen ("rock"), the latter entering the twelve-inch arena with dance re-mixes of songs such as his "Dancing In The Dark."

Despite the fact that all may be the same to the legs of the gyrating dancers on the dance floor, there still exists the tendency to want to describe musical styles in terms of one specific genre or another. Here's what producer Rick Rubin has to say on this subject:

> What makes a rock 'n' roll record is the beat, not the guitar, and what differentiates a rock record from a disco record is the kick drum (bass drum) which goes "boom ba cha boom boom ba cha" as opposed to a pulse record which goes "boom boom boom." L. L. Cool J's album is a rock 'n' roll record even though there are no guitars on it. You can make disco records and put heavy metal guitars on them, but they're still disco.

The position that it is more intelligent to be talking about today's musical genres as being defined more by the bass drum pattern than by the inclusion or exclusion of guitars is well taken. With this in mind, one would classify Madonna's "Like A Prayer" as disco, not rock, even though there are heavy guitars are up front. And in case you're wondering why Pepsi used the song to kick off a big ad campaign, the recording also features gospel singing by a full church choir. There is a little something for everybody. Perhaps one can now talk about yet another "rock" genre: Gospel-Rock! Heavens!*

For that matter, what would one make of the Bonnie Raitt tune "Think About It," for example, which includes sections played with a blues feel (complete with electric slide guitar), reggae sections, and a chorus with a hard, driving rock groove? The simple answer is that there is no pure rock, no pure disco, no pure "black" sound (with the exception of the various traditional blues styles), and no pure "white" sound. The whole here, "rock," is greater than the sum of its parts or contributing styles.

---

*The gospel influence has been heard before. In 1963, Etta James and Dinah Washington had big hits with "Pushover" and "Soulsville" respectively, combining the gospel-choir sound with the brute force of the preacher. The sound might have struck deeper had there not been the British Invasion in 1964.

Rock as a Legitimate Musical Genre

If this is the case, then how can we talk about rock as a legitimate, even distinctive musical style? In a way, it's a bit like talking about cars—there are those tiny imports and there are those whale-sized Cadillacs. They don't look the same, but they still have enough in common to be put into the same bag.

Rubin's observations that the bass-drum part generally defines the style of music are, for the most part, correct— correct, that is, if one is forced to make a decision on a song being either "rock" or "disco." But decisions like this are made on a daily basis in the entertainment industry. As an illustration of Rubin's point, just listen to rapper Tone Loc's "Wild Thing" (not a cover of the Troggs' sixties hit of the same name), his "Funky Cold Medina," or rapper Run-DMC's "Rock Box." These are rock records, black records, and dance records. Are they "disco" because they're played in discotheques? No. The beat is "rock," though the overriding sound is "black." Disco means disco music, and refers to a certain style, not a place. Furthermore, the melodies extrapolated from the raps are derived from the blues scale!

So then, it may be fair to call these tunes "black-rock- funk-blues-rap." That's about as close to the truth as one can get, yet at the same time, the term says nothing about the sound or feel of the music.

Think of music by artists like Robert Cray, one of the most prominent modern day electric blues/rock artists. "Crossover" was the word much favored in the seventies to describe songs in one genre "crossing over" from one record chart to another. Examples would be a rock tune being played on country radio (guess that makes it "country-rock," right?) and a soulful, funky tune performed by whites "crossing over" to the black radio stations' playlists. Nowadays, we hardly hear of "crossovers" any more. What has "crossed over" and merged are the very styles of music themselves, much as rock was born from country music and rhythm and blues. Today we speak about "country-rock" records rather than "country-rock crossovers." Still, the entertainment industry finds it valuable to keep track of various styles of music, which radio stations find particularly helpful in determining playlists and in charting records. In order to have a "Black Singles" chart, for example, someone must decide which records qualify as "black singles." These decisions are often arbitrary, and as they may not always be based upon musical criteria, they do little to further our discussion here. This book is concerned with the sounds of records, not the classification of records, and we have already seen that today, mixed genres is more the rule than the exception not just in the music industry, but in the way people make music.

With particular regards to arranging in the larger area of rock, producer Richard Perry addresses this very point: the blending of styles to achieve certain grooves in his records (no pun intended):

> There are no cut-and-dried rules, but there are certain sounds or techniques you can add to get a certain kind of groove. I try to mix R & B motifs into a slightly different sound, something that's not altogether pop, but not altogether rhythm and blues, either. Hopefully, it's a crossover.

Applying the above comments to our purposes here, it becomes obvious that a book on rock arranging should examine the techniques Perry talks about. The short answer to the legitimacy of rock, then, always comes back to the beat. The form or structure of most commercial rock arrangements is straight A-A-B-A or a slight variation thereof. It is the groove or feel of the particular song which bears its inclusion in one rock style or another. We will examine how the rhythm section functions in creating the basic groove to the song, as it is the groove which is most responsible for setting the style of arrangement. The choice of instrumentation depends upon what kind of feel is desired for the song. It might be very difficult for a group of Nashville studio players to create a heavy metal feel for a song—but I'd bet they'd give it a shot!

In the chapters that follow, we will look at how to arrange rock music. As we have seen, rock isn't so much a style in and of itself, but rather, it is a beat that is really set to a variety of different styles. We will first look at the blues, the grand-daddy of rock, and the music that managed to influence the greater part of American popular music in the twentieth century. Then we will look at music from the fifties, sixties, and seventies that made up rock music as a distinct entity unto itself.

From there, we will turn our attention in subsequent chapters to some of the distinct styles that characterize the contemporary rock scene, from "funk" to "heavy metal," including some genres that themselves grew out of these sounds. Though we treat these styles separately, don't let that fool you. As we have said and shown here, rock is an amalgam of sounds and styles. Your purpose as an arranger is to be a bit like a kid in a candy store: pick and choose, mix and match. If what you want is to combine a rockabilly sound with a funky groove, we'll show you how to do it. The important thing is to come up with a sound that suits what you have on hand—be it instrumentation or a particular lyric.

Another thing to remember is this: be patient. What we will be discussing in the following chapters is the work of hundreds of different musicians who have spent years racking their brains to develop their particular sounds and styles. Don't worry if your arranging doesn't work right from the start. Experiment with different beats; learn what feels good to you. Once you have that, then you will begin to master a sound that is all your own.

6

The Blues Arrangement

"...three chords, played in a repetitive style..."

We often think of pop and rock primarily as "white" music— performed by white musicians for white audiences. But it would be impossible to think of many of the styles prevailing in rock and pop today if African-Americans had not introduced the blues to the culture as a whole. From ragtime to dixieland to swing to be-bop to rock 'n' roll and even country-and-western—all of these styles owe much to this deceptively simple musical form.

There are three basic forms of the blues: eight-, twelve-, and sixteen-bar. All three are strophic—that is, they deal in verses. And all three involve the same three basic chords: I, IV, and V (technically called the "tonic," "sub-dominant," and "dominant" respectively). What these numbers and names describe are relationships between the different chords. If the tonic (I) is E, then the subdominant (IV) is five half-steps above that (A), and the dominant (V7) is two half-steps higher than the "A" (B7). Similarly, if the tonic or key of the song is G, then I, IV, and V7 are G, C, and D7 in that order.

Where the three forms differ, obviously, is in the number of measures, which are determined by the length of the line and the verse. As a result, the amount of time (in the sense of the number of measures) devoted to each of the three chords varies from one form to the next.

For our purposes here, we will speak about "blues" as a twelve-bar form, which is the most prevalent in blues and rock. It also seems to be the oldest of the blues forms, being directly related to the chants and hollers sung in the fields by the slaves brought to North America, particularly from West Africa. These chants were alternated between a "leader" and a "chorus," in which the leader called out one line and the chorus answered. Imamu Amiri Baraka, writing as LeRoi Jones in *Blues People*, describes the chants this way:

> It is easy enough to see the definite analogy between. . . a simple A-B response and a kind of song that could be developed out of it to be sung by one person, where the first line of the song is repeated twice (leader), followed by a third line (chorus). . . always a direct comment on the first two lines.

Along with the different forms—eight-bar, twelve-bar, and so on—there are also variations on how the blues are played. Originally, these were geographical styles, with fundamental differences occurring between northern and southern sounds and more subtle varieties happening between lesser regions. For example, the blues from the south incorporates what is generally known as the "country blues" style—primarily an acoustic sound, performed by a solo musician or, at most, a small group. The harmonies and rhythms tend to be simple, but with the freedom that is available only to the solo player, there is a tremendous flexibility in the use of time. The beat is not necessarily hard and fast; the rhythm tends to be more fluid.

So, when you hear the greats of the various country blues styles—musicians like Robert Johnson, Son House, Charley Patton, and so on—the thing to watch for is not so much the notes they play and the lyrics they sing, but the way in which they sing and play. Robert Johnson, perhaps the king of the Delta blues style, was not a loud or rough player. His voice was rather high, his rhythm fluctuating. In the Texas blues style, the beat is more aggressive, more pronounced, but still lighter than that found to the north, where the blues—the urban blues—developed primarily as a band music.

So, in discussing the blues as we know it today, we are really speaking of two different traditions—the country blues of the Mississippi Delta and Texas, developed and refined as an acoustic style by such musicians as Charley Patton, Robert Johnson, and Mississippi John Hurt—and the urban blues. After the emancipation of the slaves at the end of the Civil War and the outbreak of the American Industrial Revolution, many blacks headed northward to the land of opportunity and available work— in the stockyards of Kansas City, the heavy industry of such cities as Chicago, Detroit, and Gary, Indiana.

In these northern cities, the blues underwent a different sort of refinement from what had been happening in the rural south. The style became more sophisticated in terms of harmony, rhythm, and instrumentation. Acoustic guitars gave way to electrics; the harmonica made room for the sax. And solo players gave way to bands. And as the urban blues style developed, black musicians like B.B. King and Buddy Guy were drawn especially to Chicago, where they could make their music for relatively good money.

The urban blues, which provided the groundwork for the more pop-influenced rhythm 'n' blues of the early to mid-fifties, is the main source of the blues rock styles of the likes of Stevie Ray Vaughan and Robert Cray. It was also a big influence on many of the British Invasion bands of the early sixties, particularly the Rolling Stones and the Animals.

So how do the blues go? Here's a fictitious blues lyric that illustrates the twelve-bar form:

> *I was born in hard times, 1929.*
> *I was born in hard times, 1929.*
> *Had to sell an apple, just to get a dime.*

The first line of lyric here would roughly correspond to the first four measures of a twelve-bar, where the first chord (say, G7) is played. The next line would be sung over the next chord (C7) for about two measures and then the music returns to G7. Finally, the last line—a "direct comment on the first two lines," in Baraka's words—would be sung over two measures of D7, and then the music returns to the G7 again. This is outlined below.

Example 46:

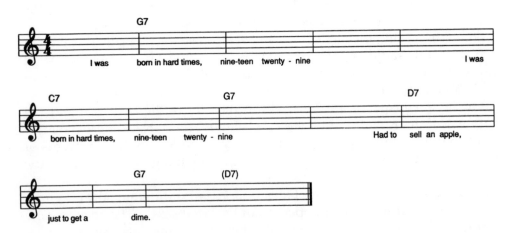

The Stones' first few albums were made up almost entirely of this kind of repertoire. The song "Heart Of Stone" is essentially a twelve-bar blues using substitute chords for those typically found in the kind of twelve-bar cited above. Here's how a chord chart to that song might look:

Example 47:

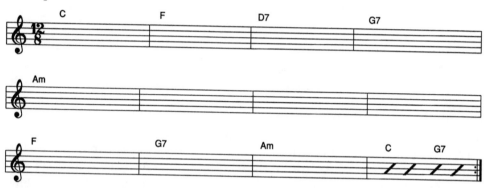

Even the Beatles were inspired by the form and feeling of the blues. The verse to their "You Can't Do That" is really a twelve-bar blues, varying only slightly from the G7-C7-G7-D7-G7 format:

Example 48:

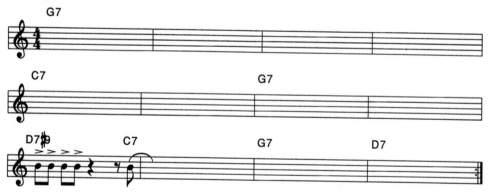

Similarly, "She's A Woman" also follows the blues structure in its verse. This is somewhat different in that the verse of the song is really a twenty-four-bar blues, with each chord being played for twice as many measures as it would in a twelve-bar blues. What follows is an outline of that twenty-four-bar ("extended twelve-bar") blues format:

Example 49:

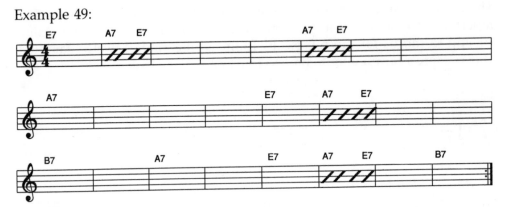

Though the twelve-bar is the norm, eight- and sixteen-bar blues forms occasionally make their way into the repertoire. A tune like Frankie Ford's "Sea Cruise" is an example of an eight-bar form which uses the same chords for both verse and chorus with a different lyric for each. The song does not have a shuffle feel (the "shuffle feel" is explained later on in this chapter) and is really a rock-blues. The chords may be written as follows:

Example 50:

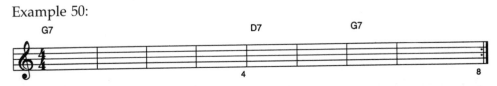

Phil Phillips' "Sea Of Love," later covered by Robert Plant and the Honeydrippers, is an eight-bar blues with a shuffle, while Jerry Lee Lewis' "Great Balls Of Fire" is another good example of an eight-bar blues.

Among the early rock'n'rollers—Elvis Presley, Chuck Berry, and Carl Perkins—the sixteen-bar blues was probably the most prevalent form. Elvis Presley's "Jailhouse Rock" is one case in point, Little Richard's "Long Tall Sally" is another.

Example 51:

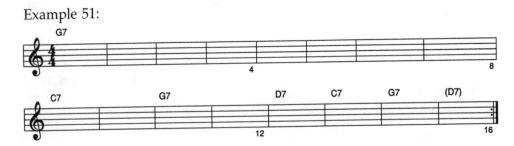

Chuck Berry's "Carol" has a bit of a twist to it, featuring a sixteen-bar verse and an eight-bar chorus. As you can see, then, the various blues forms can be modified and combined in many ways, often to great effect. The Beatles followed more pop norms by including distinct bridges—in "You Can't Do That"—and unblues-like choruses—as in "She's A Woman"—while the Stones sometimes substituted different chords for the basic I-IV-V (as in "Heart Of Stone"). But in all these cases, the blues was the kick-off point.

Lyrics in the blues often focus on the hard side of love and life: troubles with women, gambling, and liquor (not too far off the country-and-western track, for the most part); in sum, "a good feeling gone bad." This was true for much of the early rock'n'roll as well. Shoutin' Joe Turner said, "Rock 'n' roll ain't nothing but the blues pepped up"—a fairly accurate description of early and mainstream rock, before rock became stylized into various sub-genres towards the end of the sixties and into the seventies.

Even a white-boy rock-blues like "Smokin' In The Boys' Room" describes a basic sense of unhappiness, sadness, even despair. True, this lyric is trivial compared with the suffering of the African slave or the prisoner working on a prison farm, but the feeling is similar: the singer is suffering—not always about love, though love gone bad often figures in it—and it is this feeling of the unrequited, the lamented that describes the blues. Robert Cray has said that performers such as Howlin' Wolf, Robert Johnson, and B.B. King all had their own styles and tunes. But, he explains,

> It's 1985, try and do your own thing. It doesn't mean the blues have to go away—if you fall in love tomorrow and break up the next day, you're gonna have the blues. Anybody can sing the blues, you don't have to be black. . . I like to sing this music because it's about real life situations.

Blues Melodies

Blues melodies usually come from the minor pentatonic scale and are played over a succession of dominant (7th, 9th, etc.) chords. The minor pentatonic scale is also called the "blues scale" with the addition of a sixth note, the 5. In standard music notation, the C major, C minor pentatonic and C "blues" scales look like this:

Example 52:

The blues, until recently, had been regarded as a noncommercial musical style, somewhat out of step with the present day tastes—with the exceptions of anthologies and re-issues. But Robert Palmer of *The New York Times*, commenting on what he sees as the re-emergence of the blues, says:

> Young black musicians, who scorned the blues as tawdry and old-fashioned during the '60s and '70s are now forsaking disco, funk, and other commercial forms and apprenticing themselves to experienced local blues men.

All of which goes to show that while the blues may be old hat, it's a hat many people can wear comfortably.

The blues have influenced every form of popular music in America: rock, jazz, and country. When performing in any of these styles, you can draw upon the blues influence by using a riff—like the monstrous hook that opens up the Beatles' cover of the Motown hit, "Money"—or a phrase that draws upon the "blues" scale, or even a harmonic device like a chord change or turnaround. You can even write a bluesy lyric, if you happen to feel that way.

The important thing to note here is that, while it's beyond the scope of this book, a full study of the blues from its rural and urban roots will be a terrifically enriching experience, not only for your understanding of how rock music came to be the way it is, but also for your development as a musician. Robert Johnson may have been just one man with a guitar, but he could say more with three chords than you could ever possibly imagine.

Blues Arrangements

Much of today's popular music is dance music, and learning to distinguish between various rhythms can give you a clue as to what rhythmic "grooves" or "feels" are most appropriate for the various subgenres of rock. Modern blues-rock, for example, is essentially blues music played over a rock beat, with its lyrical content often derived from traditional blues themes. To begin with, we will present rhythm section variations on grooves which could be employed when arranging a blues composition. The musical role of the bass player (and we will be meaning electric bass unless otherwise specified) in playing the blues remains more or less constant from one blues feel to another. The bassist is responsible for outlining the chords in a simple, melodic manner. The general rhythmic feel of the blues is known as a shuffle, as opposed to "straight eighths" or "even eighths."

In "straight eighths," when a 4/4 measure is divided equally into eight eighth notes, each eighth note receives exactly the same amount of time. Think of "Johnny B. Goode" by Chuck Berry and "My Best Friend's Girl" by the Cars (or any song from their first album, as a matter of fact) to hear even eighth-note rhythms. However, in a shuffle rhythm, the eighth notes are not played evenly. Instead, they are broken up into uneven pairs of long and short eighths, the first being longer than the second. We usually convey the shuffle in two ways. In notation, it is typically written out as a quarter note and an eighth bracketed together with a "3" above the bracket. This is called a "broken triplet," and what that means, essentially, is that the beat, rather than being broken down into halves (in 4/4 time, eighth notes), is instead divided into the thirds. So, three eighth notes in a triplet fill the same amount of time as two regular eighth notes. Thus, in the broken triplet configuration, the quarter gets the value of two-thirds of the beat and the eighth gets the last third.

Alternately, this same uneven division of beat can be thought of as a dotted eighth note followed by a sixteenth note. When a piece is to be played as a shuffle with uneven eighths, then, you can notate in the following ways:

Example 53:

Another alternative—one that is used by many arrangers—is to write out the eighth notes evenly and put the description "shuffle" or "swing eighths" at the top of the chart. The player then chooses how much he wants the pair of eighths to swing. The true swing or shuffle feel is somewhere between the the dotted eighth and the broken triplet. It cannot be precisely notated in music and the best way to achieve the correct feel is through repeated listening and playing.

In our shuffling rhythm section, the bassist might play a pattern consisting of "uneven" or "swing" eighth notes over any given chord. Here's an example of a pattern based on the G minor pentatonic scale, played over a G7 chord. Note! Playing a minor pentatonic scale over a dominant (7th, 9th, 11th, or 13th chord) with the same root name produces the sound of the blues.

Example 54:

Often a bassist will play quarter notes when a shuffle feel is called for, though this is a "stock" pattern and it might sound clichéd. The danger with any pattern which does not vary rhythmically or melodically is that it will eventually tire the ears of the listener. The musicianship of the musician or the arranger, if a specific part is written, really comes into play in creating a musical part which fits the song just right. The bass player actually often plays rhythmic patterns that combine quarters and eighths. Here's such a pattern, with a syncopated feel created by playing on the "and" or upbeat of the second beat. This pentatonic blues riff is reminiscent of the song "Rock Me Baby" (Rod Stewart sang it as "Rock My Plimsoul" with Jeff Beck in the early seventies), an often-covered blues tune.

Example 55:

Carol Kaye has played bass on rock record dates with the Beach Boys, the Mothers of Invention, and quite literally hundreds of other performers. She says:

> (. . .) without the great musicianship of the other players involved on sessions, it would have been very hard to invent good bass lines so credit is really due the recording musicians, especially the drummers.

She continues:

> Arrangers now are also coming up with terrific ideas for bass lines. . . Soul-rock [funk] is here to stay and is. . . the biggest influence on. . . music. The electric bass plays a terrific part with all the groovy bass patterns that are possible to play on this instrument. Always listen to the relation ship of "feel" between the bass, drums, rhythm guitar and lead on a record to evaluate what pattern you should play with your group. . . everything looks hard on paper but will swing after being played a time or two.

What Carol Kaye is saying here is that the ultimate criterion for creating the "right" part is one's ear. She also places great value—and rightfully so—on one's being familiar with the music one is about to play, so that one can come up with a strong groove or feel almost instantaneously. A little thought, a little rehearsal, a little practicing always goes a long way.

Like the rock blues, the blues shuffle has a strong quarter-note feel. As we have seen elsewhere, the bass and drums establish the groove. Part of this is having the bass part playing on the beat. But another part is having the bassist play good notes on the beat—that is, notes that are in the chord (usually the root, the third, or the fifth). Passing notes—that is, notes which fall between good notes and aren't in the chords being played—should generally be kept to the offbeats.

Keep these points in mind when preparing bass charts or in giving the bassist direction in his or her playing.

The Fender bass or four-string electric bass is the instrument of choice for most bass players in all forms of contemporary popular music, be it rock, jazz, blues, country, or funk. But the majority of early rock and blues records in the fifties were recorded using an acoustic (upright or "jazz") bass, whose sound may be characterized as being fuller (having more overtones), more "natural" or "woody" and having less "punch" than its electrified counterpart.

Willie Dixon, the father of rock and blues bass, played acoustic bass on many of Chuck Berry's early cuts. His sound was more felt than heard, as the bass's function here was to keep time along with the drummer while accentuating the rhythm of the music. The acoustic bass, however, does not have the power of the electric bass, and it is more difficult to record faithfully. Most bassists switched from acoustic to electric in the early sixties. Recent developments in musical instrument technology have led to graphite basses such as the Steinberger, which have great sustain and evenness of tone across the entire range of notes. They record very cleanly with few extraneous noises or hums to complicate the job of the recording engineer. Today, one often sees multi-stringed basses such as the five-string, with a low B string, the eight-string (simply a four-string bass with doubled strings for each note), the six-string (with both an extra high and extra low string) and other hybrids. The eight-string gives a very full or "fat" sound, and has been used by John Entwhistle of the Who. Multi-stringed basses offer the musician and arranger an extended range of notes and are great for unison passages and solos. These instruments allow the bassist to play full chords, with greater ease than the traditional four string bass permits. If you are arranging for a bassist who has or has access to a multi-string bass, be aware of the extended range in either or both directions. These new instruments are becoming much more prevalent in the recording and performing industries, and their continued use will surely affect the function and sound of the electric bass.

The drummer should always complement the bassist's part in the rhythm section. Shuffles grooves should, for the most part, be kept fairly simple. Both traditional blues and rock-blues are direct, straightforward forms of expression, and the primary focus should always be on the vocalist or soloist of the moment. The band members should support the song's lyric, melody and chords in an expressive way without encroaching on the primary focus—doing what is called "overplaying." The watchword here is "less is more," and this should apply to all the musical parts. The drumbeat for a standard blues shuffle might look like this:

Example 56:

Swing eighths

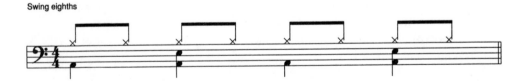

Note that the drummer here is playing the "shuffle eighths" on the hi-hat cymbals. The snare drum gets the ubiquitous 2 and 4 and the bass drum sounds on every beat—for enthusiasts, this is the "New Orleans" style. Now let's rock the beat by changing the drum beat into one more often heard on rock-blues records. Think of songs like Thin Lizzy's "The Boys Are Back In Town," Loggins and Messina's "Your Mama Don't Dance (And Your Daddy Don't Rock 'n' Roll)," and Boz Skaggs' "Lido Shuffle" to hear drum beats very much like the one notated here:

Example 57:

Swing eighths

In this example, the bass drum is the only element of the drumset playing a shuffle rhythm. Looking at this in conjunction with the previous pattern (in which the hi-hat plays the shuffle), we can conclude that it is sufficient for only one element of the drumset to feature the shuffle rhythm. For example, a "Chicago" blues shuffle has the drummer shuffling with the left hand, and is written out below. Note: this is different from what most drummers do, which is play "righthanded" or "righty." There, the right hand plays "time" on a cymbal and the left hand hits the snare.

Example 58:

Swing eighths

Now we will combine the two previous bass lines and the first two drum parts to provide the germ of a groove. Oftentimes in recording or re-hearsal situations, the drummer may actually be given a copy of the bass part. The reason is twofold: On one hand, it might be that no one involved with the arrangement knows how to write an appropriate drum chart for the song; on the other hand, a bass chart is generally enough to outline the groove to the drummer. Many drummers do prefer to have some informa-tion about the bass line's rhythmic and melodic motion. So, seeing the bass chart can help the drummer's duties tremendously. Sometimes, though, there is a very specific drum part to be played, especially in the case of a commercial spot or "jingle." Joining together the first blues shuffle bass pattern with the first shuffle drum beat gives us the groove notated here:

Example 59:

In performance, the eighth-note shuffle on the bass and the eighth-note shuffle on the hi-hat might be too overbearing for the feel, like "too much shuffling." Having the bassist play the exact same pattern but combining it with the second drum beat, in which quarter notes are played on the hi-hat, might sound more relaxed. The following is how this groove would appear in the score:

Example 60:

Suppose the bassist switches to the second shuffle rhythm, in which the "and" or upbeat of the second beat is tied to the third beat, and in which the bassist plays an eighth-note triplet on the fourth beat. If the drummer played the first drum beat, shuffling on the hi-hat, the music would look like this:

Example 61:

Here the drummer's shuffling hi-hat rhythm does not create an overbearing feel. This is because the bassist is playing a more broken-up, more interest–ing pattern rhythmically than just eighth notes; thus, there is a nice contrast between the regularity of both the eighths on the hi-hat and the quarter notes on the bass drum and the bass line. The music here does not seem to plod as much as when both players were playing every eighth-note.

There is one last permutation between the two bass lines and two drum parts which we'll examine: when the bassist plays the second, more synco-pated pattern as the drummer plays the second drum beat, with the synco-pated bass drum pattern:

Example 62:

This groove sorely needs some arranging! The bass drum and bass parts do not sound well together, because the bass drum is fighting the bass rather than working with it. The first beat is acceptable, as both instruments (looking at the bass drum as being an individual instrument) play on the first two eighth notes of the measure. However, when the bass drum is sounding with the bass on the "and of 2" in the measure, it (the bass drum) is also sounding on the third beat and its upbeat (the "and of 3"). You need to re-arrange the drummer's bass drum pattern so will it lock the bassist and drummer into the groove.

Example 63:

The drummer may even want to double-up the hi-hat rhythm, playing eighth notes instead of quarter notes. This move will not affect the groove between the bass and bass drum, and will help propel the music. The resulting bass and drum parts would look like this:

Example 64:

Bring on the Guitar!

One really can't play a convincing blues or rock-blues without a guitarist.

Let's look at some typical guitar accompaniments to the basic blues grooves outlined above. Styles of guitar accompaniment are almost as varied as individual playing styles on the instrument. Both the neophyte and studio professional might consider augmenting the bass and drums by playing a part like the one written here:

Example 65:

This is more of a rhythmic than harmonic approach to playing the groove. In other words, the guitarist here is really emphasizing the shuffling eighth-note feel rather than playing "off the chords" in the progression. Combining this with the bass and drums would yield the following:

Example 66:

It might be a good idea for the drummer now to now modify the hi-hat pattern and return to playing quarter-notes rather than eighth notes. The combination of guitar and hi-hat eighths may just be "too much" for the song. On the other hand, having the guitar and drums both play eighths, if done in a very synchronized manner, could result in a very powerful rhythm section sound. It's all up to you—the arranger—to decide which sound you prefer.

Another way in which the guitarist can contribute to the groove is by playing a chordal accompaniment. The first approach we will examine will have the guitarist play accents on various beats within the measure. The phantom guitarist in this case has already scanned the bass and drum parts and has decided to play the following accents, with a very staccato (short, clipped) feel:

Example 67:

The first "chock" or short accent reinforces the backbeat on the second beat; the second accent stands alone on the "and of 3" in the measure and thus jumps out of the music; the third accent coincides with the bass drum's accent on the "and of 4." Once again, remember to give the musician leeway in devising a unique part.

Another tack the rhythm guitarist may follow is to play chords in a more sustained, open manner, thus emphasizing the harmonic content within a rhythmic pattern. An example of this approach is notated below:

Example 68:

The two written parts above may be played with equal conviction by either the guitarist or the keyboardist. If one instrumentalist commences to play a part consisting of chordal accents (the first guitar part above), the other will naturally gravitate towards a less accented, more "open" pattern (as in the second pattern). The concept here is to avoid cluttering the arrangement —whether it is in terms of its chordal content or its rhythmic accents.

When an arranger wants the player to improvise voicings and rhythms ("comping"), the chart may consist solely of chord symbols, often with cues as to the harmonic content (voicings) and melodic direction. Here's an example of how a few measures from such a chart might look:

Example 69:

The thing for the arranger to realize here is this: Within the framework of the blues (as well as in most of rock) many different accent patterns are possible. We are simply outlining some specific parts to give you an idea of the range of possibilites.

…same three chords, different groove…

With the exception of such traditonally-based commercial blues artists as B. B. King and Robert Cray, much of what is gathered under the heading of "blues" in today's contemporary music spectrum is an amalgam of rock and roll and rhythm and blues (R & B) grooves, riffs and stylings.

Below are some approaches one might take to creating various blues-rock feels by maneuvering the bass and drum parts. Where a guitar or keyboard part is essential to the groove, it is notated below. However, the bass is the single instrument which best and most fully conveys the germ or essence of the groove, and, combined with the drumbeat, really leads the other players towards their respective parts in an impromptu arrangement. Here's something else to think about in your arranging: When the music includes a repeating riff or melodic line, try having various instruments play it. Have the second guitar, for example, "double" (play the exact same thing simultaneously) a keyboard line in a different octave (up higher or down lower). Or, if a song has a very recognizable bass part, try incorporating musical morsels of it in your arrangement.

Example 70:

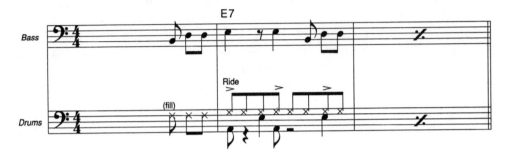

This groove might bring to mind "Born In Chicago" (popularized in the late sixties by the Paul Butterfield Blues Band), or, if altered slightly as below, something reminiscent of the tune "Oh, Pretty Woman"—not Roy Orbison's song, but the blues standard recorded by Albert King.

Example 71:

Were the guitar part changed to accents on 2 and 4, the listener might be reminded of Albert King's "Born Under A Bad Sign." That song has a particularly strong 2 and 4 feel, and a rhythm chart for the tune might look like this:

Example 72:

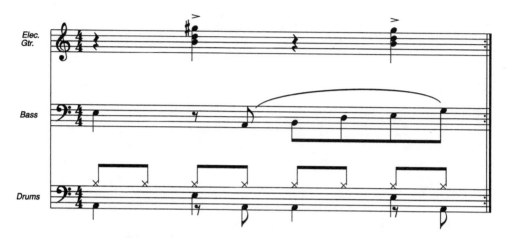

Often blues tunes are based on derived from a certain riff or musical phrase. Usually, when this is the case, the riff is repeated throughout the song. "Born Under A Bad Sign" and "Oh, Pretty Woman" are two good examples of this.

Furthermore, the riff sometimes continues throughout the song. Then it is called an *ostinato* (see the Appendix). A simple, repeating riff which illustrates this concept is the lick from "I'm A Man":

Example 73:

Or, how about the riff from "Mustang Sally," an extended 24-bar blues?

Example 74:

Though they are not technically "ostinato" phrases since they do not occur throughout the song, listen to these three songs to get a better understanding of this concept: Jimi Hendrix's "Foxey Lady," the Stones' "Last Time," and the Beatles' "Day Tripper."

Example 75:

Example 76:

Example 77:

After studying these examples, you might begin thinking about what gives a certain performer or instrumentalist his or her own distinctive "style." When various members of a band have already created styles of their own and consistently play that way within a group, that band would tend to have a sound of its own based upon the combining of individual styles. A good example of this is the now-defunct New York R & B group Stuff, which was simply a rhythm section, often with a lead vocalist or horn player up front. Rhythm and blues, gospel, jazz, and rock elements were personified by such guitarists as Cornell DuPree and Eric Gale; such drummers as Chris Parker, Steve Gadd, and Richard Crooks; such pianists as Richard Tee; and bassists like Gordon Edwards. Similarly, when an artist records with the same musicians time after time, the band's contribution to the sound of the artist can be tremendous. Perhaps one of the best examples of this is the way in which guitarist Scotty Moore, bassist Bill Black, and drummer D. J. Fontana helped to create the sound of Elvis Presley's early Sun recordings.

The same is true with repertoire, arranging and producing. That is why one may hear of a "Phil Spector" sound, a "Steely Dan-like" song and a "Duke Ellington-ish" arrangement. Some of the musical elements which are responsible for giving music a recognizable sound of its own are: the repertoire, the performer, the band or musicians, the arrangement of material and the recording of the material (including production). Here we are only dealing with arranging, but it's important to see the larger picture: arrange all you will but the sound of Def Leppard backing Perry Como singing "I Shot The Sherriff" as arranged by Mantovani and produced and recorded by Phil Spector may not lead to a convincing musical conclusion and may indeed lack any semblance of style. On the other hand, repeated listenings to records by performers like the Who, the Stones, the Eagles, James Brown, David Bowie, and Talking Heads are hardly necessary for one to be able to perceive each performer's unique style. For each artist's recordings mentioned above, there is a consistency throughout in terms of their choice of repertoire, the sound of their music and vocals, the arrangement of their material, and the methods of production and recording used in making their records.

7

The Rock and Rhythm 'n' Blues Arrangement

April, 1958: Elvis Presley was inducted into the Army and "Volare" topped the charts as the number-one song of the year. There was no unified "rock" sound, no backbeat thud until 1964, the year of...well, soon enough. Before then, in 1956, Elvis had made history with "Heartbreak Hotel," the first single to top simultaneously the Pop, Country, and Rhythm & Blues charts. No one knew it then, but this strange crossover phenomenon was to provide the real recipe for rock as we understand the term today.

In the following years, Elvis never really developed into the rocking rock star he could have became—largely because of manager Colonel Tom Parker's limited musical vision and monopolistic direction.

Elvis' hits through 1960 included the eight-bar, 12/8 blues-styled "One Night," the "O Sole Mio" ripoff "It's Now Or Never," and the torchy "Are You Lonesome Tonight?" The once and future King of Rock was recording very derivative material. During the same period, America made big hits out of nice, safe songs like "Pink Shoelaces," "The Three Bells" and "Theme From A Summer Place."

By 1962, however, the record charts were peppered with heavier sounds like "He's a Rebel," "The Locomotion," and "Do You Love Me." The rhythm 'n' blues influence was creeping into the radios and jukeboxes of whitebread America. While the average malted-sipping teen most probably wasn't aware that the term "juke" derives from the slang for a southern roadhouse (the "juke joint"), by 1963 he or she was moving to the beat of the soul-infected "Louie Louie," Stevie Wonder's "Fingertips (Part II)," "He's So Fine," "Da Doo Ron Ron," "You Really Got a Hold on Me," "Tell Him," "Mama Didn't Lie" and "Be My Baby." As Old Blue Eyes, Frank Sinatra, was to sing later, "It was a very good year."

February, 1964: For serious fans of music history, it really begins with a little article in the back pages of *The New York Times* in October, 1963—an amusing piece about the wave of hysteria sweeping Britain called "Beatle-mania." It was filler material, and not news, because everybody knew that the British had never done anything over here. Why, the Beatles had released several singles already in America and nothing had happened. Then, after much thought (for that read "many corporate decisions") Capitol-EMI decided to promote the band, maybe even sponsor a tour. First thing, though, was to get them onto the *Ed Sullivan Show.*

Enter the Beatles. In 1964 alone, they had number-one hits with "I Want To Hold Your Hand," "She Loves You," "Please, Please Me," "Do You Want To Know A Secret?" and "Can't Buy Me Love." While Chuck Berry had had chart hits dating back to the mid-'50s (as did many other rock 'n' rollers), he was still sharing pop airtime with "Cherry Pink And Apple Blossom White."

In 1964, though, the top 100 were almost entirely made up of songs which had a unified sound about all of them! The quintessential 2 and 4 rock backbeat is nowhere better displayed than in Martha and the Vandellas's "Dancing In The Streets," also a 1964 chartbuster. Side by side with both R & B and the Beatles were songs in yet a new style of rock—the California-inspired "surf" music-by artists like the Beach Boys (who had actually hit one year earlier with "Surfin' U.S.A."), Ronnie and the Daytonas, Jan and Dean, and the Hondells. So, dating back to its very roots, rock has always had a synthetic and democratic quality.

So what were the elements of the early rock sound? To give you a first-hand look at the roots of rock and roll in terms of arranging, we'll now look at some typical arrangements in the rockabilly and early R & B styles. A basic understanding of the most salient features of these genres will help you in creating an arrangement in a particular style and groove and learning to blend elements from different rock genres to create a distinctive sound.

Rockabilly, born from the two seemingly unrelated styles of white country music and black rhythm and blues, is rock's most direct forebearer. The similarities between the two account for the special quality of rock music. The rhythm of authentic rockabilly music is primarily the shuffle, the "swing eighth"* though it's interesting to note that the more "rocky" of both the traditional and modern-day rockabilly artists gravitate towards the straight-eighth feel in their music. Such examples as Buddy Holly ("Rave On"), The Rock and Roll Trio ("Train Kept A-Rollin'"), Jerry Lee Lewis ("Great Balls Of Fire," "Whole Lotta Shakin' Goin' On"), and Dave Edmunds come to mind.

---

*Please see the chapter "The Blues Arrangement" above for a discussion of swing eighths.

Here's a few measures of "Save The Last One For Me," arranged in a rocka-billy shuffle feel:

Example 78:

One of the first things to note about this "adaptation" is the time signature: 4/4. Traditional bluegrass and country music is written in straight 2/4 time, not as a shuffle. The two main rhythmic differences between country and rockabilly are the strong backbeat and the swing feel. The two also diverge in the area of tempo. Rockabilly is truly "pepped up" country, and its generally quick tempos set it apart from its ancestors.

Note that the bass is "walking" and the guitar accents are similar to those in a standard blues-shuffle. The drummer is playing a shuffle beat and the keyboardist a triplet rhythm, which nicely contrasts with the other bandmembers' eighths. The pianist could also "tinkle" with the right hand. Basically if this tune were slowed down, we'd have the chorus to "Ain't That A Shame"!

How about doing the same tune in a more straightforward, pulsing rock groove, while preserving the rockabilly quality?

Example 79:

Now the guitarist is doing the "walking," a la Duane Eddy. He is processing his signal by using a delay box that provides an intense reverberant sound. (The kind of guitarist who goes for the sound of tube amps would go for an

Echoplex—a dinosaur today, but which was the state of the art only 20 years ago). This adds an echo strongly associated with the style. The keyboardist is comping in a manner similiar to that of the guitarist in the previous example, and the bassist and drummer are each playing a basic rock beat: beats 2 and 4 on the snare and eighth notes on the bass. A second guitar has been added to play bluesy fills in the style of Scotty Moore (Elvis' original lead picker), Les Paul, and Carl Perkins. The cardinal rockabilly fill goes like this:

Example 80:

To show you how it's just one short step from here to a post-Beatles hard rock groove, let's have the bassist and guitarist switch parts (the bassist is walking with straight eighths and the guitarist is playing a pulsing straight eighth-note part), have the second guitarist return to accents in the style of the keyboardist's former part, and have the keyboard player turn up all of the amps to 10 and then go out for refreshments. Here's what it would look like on paper, staying on one chord:

Example 81:

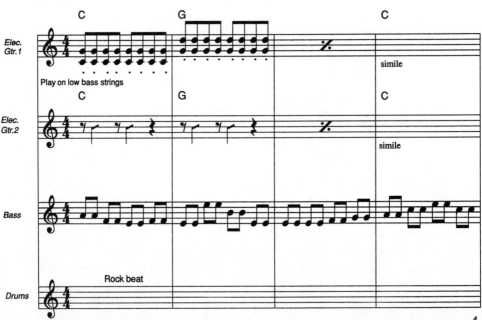

What it would sound like is T-Rex's "Bang-A-Gong," the seminal rock classic by the late Marc Bolan. Perhaps the most important step in deriving this arrangement was performed by the keyboardist, who didn't actually play on the number but had an equally important duty: turning up the amps! Ah, yes, the sweet sound of volume! It's almost magical how with one swift flick of the wrist and a slight change in rhythm we can span decades of rock styles and create a real kickin' groove. The biggest hits of 1958 included the following songs, all built upon a strong four-beat groove, and more than a few owing a debt to the blues: "At The Hop," "Bird Dog," "Splish Splash," "Sweet Little Sixteen," "Do You Want To Dance?" and "Rebel Rouser." That obsessive volume and incessant, pulsing beat, forever provoking the ire of elders throughout the generations, were here to stay.

The amalgam known as rock drew heavily upon rhythm and blues influences in its path to creation and maturity. As we have seen, the blues, particularly with its chordal and rhythmic motifs, had a tremendous influence on the development of rock while remaining a separate style. So, let's return to yesteryear's hit records and see how rock influenced the blues to create the loosely-defined R & B style itself, and how this sub-genre became a primary force in rock music.

In the fifties, doo-wop or street-corner singing was a popular pastime of both blacks and whites in the urban areas of the United States. The feel or rhythm was basically that of the 12/8 blues, epitomized by records like "Only You," "Earth Angel," and the already noted "Ain't That A Shame." However, a new pulse, a new rhythm was added to the standard blues arrangement of the time. Bo Diddley's "Bo Diddley" hit the charts in mid-1955, with its characteristic rhythm:

Example 82:

played over the chords of the blues, the I-IV-V progression.

Over the next few years, tunes such as "Let The Good Times Roll," "Speedo," "I'm Walkin," "Get A Job," and "Yakety Yak" exemplified the rhythmic approach to the I-IV-V progression and the various combinations and permutations of chords. Following are some of the syncopated grooves to a few of the above examples:

Example 83:

"I'm Walkin"

Example 84:

"Get A Job"

The rhythmic factor was strengthened over the next few years. In 1961, the Miracles had a hit with "Shop Around," which provides a great example of an early R & B bass line:

Example 85:

Interestingly enough, the bassline to Gene McDaniels' "One Hundred Pounds of Clay" (another hit from 1961) employs almost the exact same rhythmic properties as that from "Shop Around":

Example 86:

What is characteristic about these bass parts is not the bass part itself, but how it interlocks with the rest of the rhythm section. The core of R & B is the rhythmic counterpoint between the musical parts, and this counterpoint starts with the bass and drums. We know how important it is for the drummer's bass drum foot to be locked in with the bassist's rhythm.

In the early sixties, Motown featured R & B with such artists as the Miracles, the Temptations, Marvin Gaye, Stevie Wonder, Martha and the Vandellas, the Four Tops, and the Supremes, making this "groove" the primary focus of the music. Motown's straightforward drumming with the heavy backbeat on 2 and 4 gave the bassist (most often James Jamerson) lots of freedom to improvise funky, syncopated bass lines over fairly simple chord progressions. The groove in the following example is so strong that should even a solo acoustic guitar or piano play the chords in the rhythm notated, a musically knowledgeable person would undoubtedly reply "Heat Wave" if questioned about the song's identity:

Example 87:

The same instantly identifiable quality exists with the bass and drum parts to the Ronettes' "Be My Baby":

Example 88:

What producer Phil Spector did here was to tailor the music of black R & B artists to his own personal vision and sound, resulting in some of the most unique and powerful rock music ever recorded. His arrangements included multiple tracks of guitar, keyboard, percussion, and vocals to create his famous "Wall of Sound." Listen to Ike and Tina Turner's "River Deep, Mountain High" as an example.

Just as we arranged "Save The Last One For Me" as a rockabilly tune, let's give it a try as an R & B flavored tune. Put on your dancin' shoes, and here we go:

Example 89:

The bass and drum are naturally "locked in" with one another and as one electric guitar plays a funky, syncopated rhythm (using partial chords and not those big, powerful root-fifth "heavy" chords), the other plays a muted, syncopated single-note pattern. The purpose here is to have all the parts lock in and create the effect of notes bouncing back and forth off of one another.

Many R & B and Motown tunes of the mid- to late sixties included within them elements of the driving, hard rockin' songs derived from the rockabilly influence. A tune like "Stop, In The Name Of Love" contrasts a pulsing, eighth-note bass part in the chorus (courtesy, as always, of James Jamerson), which actually opens the song with a broken eighth-note rhythm in the verse. Here's a pattern similar to what Jamerson plays in this song:

Example 90:

Interestingly enough, the top song of 1966, "Sunny," used this same bass line over a series of chords—II-V—usually associated with pop standards and jazz. The charts for that year, however, were inundated with bands whose names began with "the," and for the most part, they were the bands of the British Invasion and their American imitators. To wit: the Beatles, the Mamas and Papas, the Association, the Troggs, the Hollies, the Monkees, the Byrds, the Rolling Stones, the Righteous Brothers, the Vogues, the Mindbenders, the Dave Clark Five, the Young Rascals, the Cyrkle, and the Lovin' Spoonful.

At about this time in music there arose a new crop of white singers who sang "soul" music; their music was referred to by the somewhat derogatory name of "blue-eyed soul." The best-known of these were the Young Rascals and the Righteous Brothers.

"Soulful" singing cannot be precisely defined, but can be partially decribed as a vocal with a strongly emotional delivery and a reliance on "blue" notes and the blues scale. There is a strong association here with gospel music and the plaintive traditional blues. A "blue-eyed soul" singer whose work spans decades of rock is Steve Winwood, whose "Roll With It" draws upon the great R & B grooves of the sixties (when he himself was singing with the Spencer Davis Group). In fact, as you listen to Winwood's song, try to identify the various grooves and parts, and to which songs they pay tribute.

If, as some have said, Rock 'n' Roll died in 1967, then R & B and "soul" surely took over some of its power and popularity. In that year, more than in any single year previous, our ears drew closer to the sounds of R & B through songs like Aretha's "Respect" and "Baby I Love You," Stevie's "I Was Made To Love Her," Sam and Dave's "Soul Man," "Gimme Little Sign," "Sweet Soul Music," Wilson Pickett's "Funky Broadway," the Four Tops' "Bernadette," and Marvin and Tammi's "Ain't No Mountain High Enough." Even Bill Cosby hopped on the soultrain with "Little Ole Man" as did Johnny Rivers with his cover of "Baby I Need Your Lovin'."

And while the bassist—hate to say it again, but probably James Jamerson —was thumping along, how was the guitarist contributing to the groove? In "Respect," one electric guitar plays a straightforward rhythm on the down-beats as the other plays the lead line. Note that the bass here is playing a very syncopated rhythm utilizing broken sixteenth notes. Bass parts by the late sixties were becoming more funky, getting into the area of sixteenth notes, allowing the bassist to get funky in a way that eighth notes do not allow (funk will be discussed in the next chapter). Here'a rhythm chart that works well with a song like "Respect":

Example 91:

The straight rhythm guitar here emphasizes the downbeat, in contrast to the other musicians' syncopated parts. Guitar has a similar role in the arrangement of "Gimme Little Sign," in which the piano plays the fills.

Example 92:

Different tune, same kind of groove: the guitar treatment to "I Was Made To Love Her":

Example 93:

Another way in which the electric guitar fits into the R & B framework is by playing a part which is neither full chords nor a single-note line. What we are talking about here is a part using two notes ("double stops") or partial chords. The two names who specialize in this style of playing are Steve Cropper and Cornell Dupree, and here's something similar to what Cropper plays on "Soul Man," followed by a guitar part like the one heard on "Funky Broadway."

Example 94:

Example 95:

It's important to once again remember that this kind of guitar playing is largely improvised by the musician, who is more often that not merely looking at a basic chord chart: C, Am, F, G7, and so on. The "interlocking parts" concept displayed in most R & B reached its height by 1975, in works by bands such as Earth, Wind and Fire and the Average White Band. As we shall see later, practically every sixteenth note was accounted for in some way throughout songs like "Pick Up The Pieces" and "Shining Star." Throughout the late sixties, the only real rocking music to hit the charts came mostly from—you guessed it—the Beatles and the Stones. Sure, there were occassional exceptions by bands like the Doors and Steppenwolf, and by 1972 the "Second British Invasion" had arrived with the likes of Rod Stewart, Free, T-Rex, Badfinger, and the Sweet. Not to mention groups like Mott the Hoople, the Strawbs, and Slade, who, although not chart-busters, certainly had widespread followings and sold thousands of albums.

In order for you to get a feel for how the rest of this book proceeds, through funk, reggae, disco, hard rock, heavy metal and "new wave," let's take a brisk walk through the music of the seventies to see which musical styles and trends were developing and which were dissolving. Mellow

BUSINESS REPLY MAIL

FIRST CLASS   PERMIT NO. 300   LAKEWOOD, N.J.

Postage will be paid by

Watson-Guptill Publications

1515 Broadway
New York, New York 10109-0025

Your opinion of this book would be most helpful to us. Please take a moment to fill out this card.

Title: _____ Author _____

_____

What did you like (or not like)? _____

_____

What did you find most useful? _____

_____

_____

Bought at _____ Please initial if you can be quoted _____

_____ Your profession _____

Would you like a FREE catalog of all our publications? ☐ Yes ☐ No

I am primarily interested in ☐ art instruction (AB WG00)
                              ☐ graphic design (DB GD00)
                              ☐ architecture/interior design (DB WH00)
                              ☐ photography (PB AM00)
                              ☐ music (MB BB00)

Name _____

Address _____

City/State/Zip _____

sounds, funky sounds, country sounds, rock sounds were all present in the music of the time. Not particularly a "musicians' decade," the seventies gave us the emotional equivalents to 1955's "Cherry Pink And Apple Blossom White," "Tie A Yellow Ribbon...," "You Light Up My Life," "Close To You," "Billy Don't Be A Hero"...enough said. All the while, some new sounds were to be heard, if you listened carefully. The major trend of the decade was disco, and that went hand-in-hand with its two most successful proponents, the Bee Gees and Donna Summer. A strange, foreign beat was heard on Stevie Wonder's "Boogie On, Reggae Woman" and a new artist, hailed as the New Elvis, appeared on the scene. His name was David Bowie, and he brought well, some "changes" to the music scene.

The seventies ended on an dreary note: "My Sharona" topped *Billboard's* Top 100 for the year 1979. With respect to the technology at the time, the performance, the hooks, the arrangement, and all of the other elements which go into making a hit record, it was the "perfect" single. But something was missing. The fire that sparked rock, whether in the form of rock and roll or R & B, was gone. Something had to happen, and it did. The logical conclusion to the middle-of-the-road attitude of the seventies was a return to basics, to rock and blues. As the rock grew into the "new wave" and metal of the eighties, the natural offshoot of R & B was a funkier music, played with an intensity equal to that of James Brown. So now let's see how greatly the sound of an arrangement can be changed by manipulating the rhythms and finding a new groove.

8

The Funk Arrangement

The melding of rock and funk has reached its current zenith through the music of Prince, perhaps the most distinctive stylist to hit the music scene since David Bowie. Prince can rock hard, as evidenced by "Little Red Corvette," or can funk furiously, as in his "1999" and "Kiss." Curiously, "Kiss" was covered by Tom Jones with the Art of Noise. Throughout the eighties, Jones was perceived as a lounge-lizard dinosaur, a throwback to the era when his contemporaries included middle-of-the-road singers like Englebert Humperdinck. Not too funky, and definitely not rock. As we've mentioned earlier, an artist's style and perceived image are usually closely associated with their repetoire. By covering Prince's tune, Tom Jones gave himself a new musical life, as it were, which even included a frequently rotated music video on the music television stations. As we compared different arrangements of "Jump" and "Viva Las Vegas," let's do the same with "Kiss." Bear in mind that Prince's arrangements are often radical in terms of instrumentation and vocals. At times in his music, the bass part is barely audible, his vocals sometimes include high-pitched screams (a la James Brown) and guttural grunts in the style of Sly Stone, and live drumming is often replaced by its hi-tech equivalent, the drum machine.

Furthermore, traditional "solo" sections are often absent and the groove sometimes switches from funk to rock and back again. Check out his "Batdance" for a good example of this blending of genres within a single piece. In much of today's music, the groove is often eclectic, and there is no better practitioner of this than Prince.

Now on to "Kiss." The form or structure of both versions is identical: verse, verse, solo section, verse, and then out. The tune is based on a blues progression, but each verse is 28 measures, as follows:

8 bars:	I chord (all chords are dominant—7th, 9th, etc.)
4 bars:	IV chord
4 bars:	I chord
2 bars:	V chord
2 bars:	IV chord
2 bars:	V chord
1 bar:	IV chord
1 bar:	V chord
4 bars:	I chord
28 bars:	Total

Now that we know something about the chord progressions and form of the blues, we may ask ourselves the following question: is this tune a blues, a rock blues? Not exactly. A funk blues? Absolutely, positively, yes! The melody relies heavily upon the minor pentatonic scale with its "blue" notes and though the standard eight-, twelve-, or sixteen-measure form has been enlarged upon, the I-IV-V progression is still the palette for the chords in "Kiss."

But why did Prince not follow a traditional blues format in "Kiss"? The answer is that the lyric for each verse (note!— there is no distinct "chorus" to the song) is longer and requires more measures of music for its exposition than a standard blues progression supplies. We don't know whether the music or the lyric was written first, but here is a plausible explanation: the groove came first, then the lyric and its melody. Once it was established, the groove was played over the various chords which go with the melody line. Then, when the lyric was completed, so were the chord changes, and this process took 28 measures.

Tom Jones' version is in a C blues tonality, while Prince sings and plays in the A blues tonality. This difference is probably because of the different vocal ranges of the two singers, and is not a ramification of the differing effects of the two arrangements. One is used to hearing Jones' deeper voice and Prince's falsetto (see Appendix). The fact here is that Prince is singing higher than Jones—his A is higher than Jones' C, not lower. Remember, the notes exist in a continuum, so we cannot say that "A is of a lower pitch than C." The question is which A? In which range? In this case, it is the A above C.

How about the tempo and the dynamics? Jones' "Kiss" is the more lively of the two, its tempo equal to a metronome setting of about 120, while Prince's clocks in at about 112.

This is a significant difference, one that is felt immediately. The slower version feels like a medium slow-funk groove, and the peppier version feels like a funk-pop tune. Noted New York arranger Steve Tarshis holds the view that tempo—setting the tempo, that is—is the most crucial part of creating an arrangement that works for the song, the artist and the audience. He believes that adjusting the tempo can make something work which did not work at a different speed.

Furthermore, Tarshis says that different tempos can dictate or suggest various musical ideas. Two examples: a quicker tempo may cause the bass player to play sparser than he or she would at a slower tempo, and a horn line that sounded lethargic when played slowly may sound better at a faster tempo. In the first case, the actual musical part changes with the changing tempo; in the second, a part which may have been eliminated at a slow tempo feels appropriate at a faster one. Of course, the opposite is true as well.

In general, songwriters tend to hear their music too slowly—that is, the tempo at which they "hear" their own songs is often slower than they should be played—recall the case of John Lennon. Often the first comment heard in a band rehearsal of a new song is, "It's too slow." What is the right tempo? Sometimes exact opposites may work in choosing a tempo, like speeding up what was thought of a slow song or playing a fast song as a ballad. The effect can be dramatic, and, more importantly, the song may work at the new tempo. A great example of this in the rock repertoire is Bruce Springsteen's "Rosalita," originally a ballad—ballads are usually fairly slow in tempo—which was recorded at a much faster tempo than Springsteen had initially envisioned. And, of course, the previously mentioned ballad-turned-pop/rock "Please, Please Me" by the Beatles.

So, it's wise to get the right tempo first. It may save you hours of "re-arranging" the other elements of your tune, and you may find that it was only the tempo that needed to be changed in the first place!

Onto dynamics: Prince's "Kiss" does not stray much from one dynamic level—there are no particularly loud or soft parts, and no areas of crescendo or diminuendo. Tom Jones' arrangement, on the other hand, is more developed dynamically, due to the added presence of a horn section and the "stacked" method of orchestration employed. The horns' fills and crescendos add lots of interest to the arrangement, as does the up-front lead guitar. This brings us to an important point regarding the concept underlying each arrangement, and how all other facets of a good arrangement follow the "concept."

A successful arranging concept should be a logical extension of the artist's musical and personal image and style, and such is the case with both versions of "Kiss." Prince's recording is based upon the concept of a "riff" tune, a "rhythm groove," similar to the kinds of things that James Brown did in the sixties and seventies, like his "Cold Sweat" and "Hot Pants." In Prince's version of "Kiss," the keyboard plays the main riff accompanied by the bass and drum machine. The bass is way back in the mix, and is very dead sounding, its pitch implied and felt more than heard. The music track is almost as sparse as a rap or hip-hop track; in fact, Prince's use of rhythms parallels the use of funky multi-rhythms in rap music. It's a dance track, all in all, and the focus seems to be on the unique vocal stylings and lyric, as well as on the groove itself. The following bass groove closely resembles that used in both versions:

Example 96:

Prince's drum track uses a broken sixteenth-note hi-hat pattern while Jones' drum track is straight eighths.

Example 97:

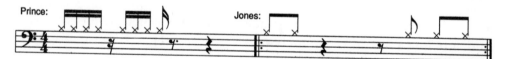

The keyboard plays a riff throughout Prince's first two verses and in the third, the funky rhythm guitar is added. Jones' version opens with sparse funky guitar and bass, then keyboards, backup vocals, horns, and percussion are all added during the first verse. The more "standard" of the two arrangements, Jones' "Kiss" includes a single-note lead guitar solo between the second and third verses; Prince includes a short rhythm guitar solo and a short lead in the same place in his version.

Here are some funky, broken sixteenth patterns used in "Kiss":

Example 98:

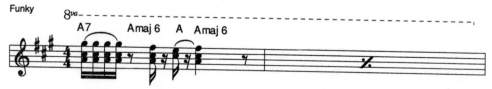

Example 99:
Keyboard:

So, it seems as if Tom Jones copped Prince's basic groove but sped it up, expanded upon the instrumentation (bringing his sound nearer to that of the usual full band recording) and changed the dynamics to make his record more "pop" than "funk." All of his parts balance nicely and provide a varying focus for the arrangement; listener interest is unflagging.

Has Tom Jones done a better job than Prince in arranging "Kiss"? Not if you have been following the gist of this book, he hasn't. Prince created the record he wanted in terms of his concept, his vision, and Tom Jones did the same. Prince's "Kiss" was a huge hit, the #19 record of 1986 according to *Billboard*, so his arrangement must have been appreciated by lots of folks. And Tom Jones' version is no more or less successful just because it is more pop-oriented.

The irony here is that Prince's spacy arrangement of "Kiss" was the "bigger" hit of the two. We can see how the distinction between what is "commercial" and what is not is lessening. Songs don't have to follow "stock" arrangements anymore, and, in fact, they don't even have to have clear cut or infinitely repeated chorus sections to be viable products.

We can all only hope that this liberalized climate will continue and foster increased creativity and experimentation among composers, musicians, arrangers, and producers.

Okay, now you know what funky is—just take some sixteenth-notes, break 'em, and mix them up, right? Well, sort of, but it's not quite as simple as just that. There must be some degree of rhythmic counterpoint between the parts, and that is often a matter which is left up to the individual musicians. It's worth mentioning here the way in which many black gospel and R & B groups go about creating their parts, their "arrangements." Just listen to the rhythmic counterpoint of the parts in a gospel church choir to get a real feel for what we mean by parts locking in with one another. Sections seem to bounce off one another, creating what is essentially a musical dialogue.

The communal approach to the R & B arrangement is to have all of the participants come together and actually work out their parts. As she did while a youngster singing in church, Aretha Franklin uses this same "sit down, and let's get our parts" approach in her music today, as do many other artists, including the infamous Fruithead and her group. This approach seems to easily lead to a natural counterpoint between parts, for if the part feels right, it usually is right for the song.

It takes lots of familiarity with many different kinds of grooves as well as practice in writing out parts in order to create a funky groove in the absence of musicians to actually play and try out the parts. However, let's say you have to come up with a funky groove to a tune and no one's around for you to have your human sounding board. We'll start out by getting a thing going between the bass and drums:

Example 100:

Now, let's add a rhythm guitar, something really high-end sounding—played on, say, a twangy, trebly guitar like a Fender Telecaster:

Example 101:

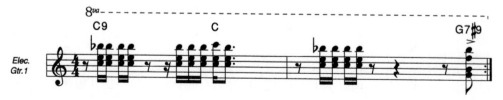

Notice that the guitar is playing on beats on which the bass is not playing, leading to a see-saw countrapuntal motion between the two parts. How about a second guitar part to complement the first? The second guitarist might play something like the following:

Example 102:

Now that we have the groove, its tightness will depend on how accurately the players play their respective parts. Should we want to change the feel in, say, the chorus or bridge of the song, we may have the players play something like the following, in which the drummer is a bit more driving, the bass a bit more pumping (following the drum part) and the guitars less syncopated. One guitar will play a more constant, full part and the other will accent 2 and 4 along with the snare:

Example 103:

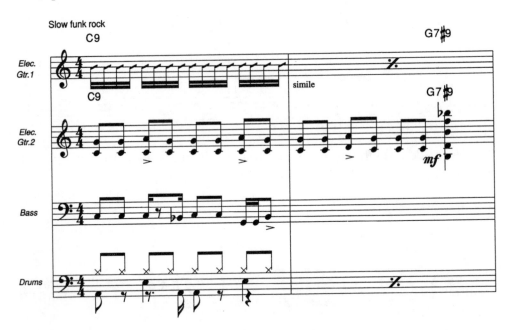

This will still sound syncopated and funky, but will be a bit more "rocky" than pure funk, thanks to the now driving rhythm section. Examples of changing the groove in a funk tune abound in the rock repertoire; a shining example is INXS' tune "What You Need." The verse groove can be pretty much accounted for by the bass and two guitar parts. They sound something like this:

Example 104:

At a certain point in the song, the music becomes much more driving and powerful, as the bass and drums change to a straight eighth-note part in conjunction with the guitar. They play this for eight measures, all the while increasing in force and volume—a long crescendo—and this has the effect of adding a real sense of dynamics to the song. At the end of the buildup, the musicians return to the original groove.

Reggae

The people of the Caribbean nations have developed various and unique musical styles, all based upon some degree of syncopation. The best known of these is reggae, and some of its best-known proponents are the late Bob Marley, Peter Tosh, the Wailers, Toots and the Maytals, and Jimmy Cliff. We'll talk about some of the characteristics of the reggae groove from the standpoint of what the various musicians play.

To some, reggae sounds like "backwards" music, perhaps because the first strong accent of the measure often occurs on the first beat, and we are used to hearing the "thud" of rock on the second and fourth beats. Reggae has been described as a "half-time shuffle turned around," which means that the first beat is now the second beat and so on. But just as there are lots of different rock and R & B grooves, so there are many different reggae grooves. All reggae is not slow, and all does not sound like a backwards halftime shuffle.

Following are a couple of different reggae grooves which will start getting you familiar with this Carribean "funk." We'll start with a kind of hybrid rock-reggae groove, not exactly Jamaican in nature, but the kind of feel that Stevie Wonder used on "Boogie On Reggae Woman." In this groove, the drum plays pretty much a straight rock beat, with a sixteenth-note pattern on the hi-hat. So, we now know that it's not the drum beat alone which makes reggae, but the interplay between the parts.

Example 105:

Contrast the above with the groove to a true Jamaican reggae tune like "This Is Reggae Music" by Zap Pow:

Example 106:

This shows two important stylistic points about authentic reggae: the "skank" beat (what they call "shank" in London) which the guitar plays and the very sparse yet powerful bass part. Reggae in general adheres to the dictum "less is more," proving that the groove can indeed be created by just a few instruments which are locked in. The above groove can be used for, say, "I Shot The Sheriff," probably the most widely known reggae tune, and it would sound just fine. Take the same groove, slow it down to a tempo equal to a metronome setting of about 54, and the resulting feel is heavy and ponderous, definitely not upbeat and carefree.

So, we see that a simple change in one of the rhythm section parts or a change of tempo can drastically alter the feel of a reggae tune.

Returning to a moderate tempo of about mm=80, let's rearrange the drum pattern and the bass pattern to create a piece of music which is still in the reggae vein yet feels more bouncy, more "pop." How can we accomplish this? Well, let's start by writing a more moving bassline, something syncopated and funky, which doesn't sound quite so bulky. Something like this, and note the staccato "dots" under the noteheads, giving a clipped feel to the notes:

Example 107:

Let's have the guitar keep playing the "skank" or upbeat rhythm, to keep that unique reggae element present. This adds a very hip element of rhythmic counterpoint to the new bass line, as many of the guitar accents come in on beats during which the bassist is resting.

And to move the drum beat slightly closer to a rock-pop feel, we will now arrange the drum beat so that the snare is sounded on—you guessed it—two and four of each measure. The drummer's hi-hat is fine the way it is, sounding with the guitar's skanks, and the bass drum pattern, while not following the bass rhythm exactly, does sound on some of the same beats. The resulting rhythm section groove will now propel the tune quite nicely, and it will still sound like reggae.

An important thing to remember here is that the concept of locking in between the bass and drums does not mean that each of these instruments should always be sounding together! If the drummer in the last example sounded his or her bass drum everywhere that the bass played a note, the groove would, strangely enough, lose prominence and strength, not gain it. Try it in your own arrangements, and doubtless you will see that, once again, less is more where grooves are concerned.

Disco

Though the disco craze reached its modern peak with the Bee Gee's soundtrack to *Saturday Night Fever*, many of the rhythms and grooves associated with this rock sub-genre have made their way into the mainstream, and it behooves the aspiring arranger to have a familiarity with at least some of them.

Today, as twenty years ago (come to think of it, didn't someone once say that rock would "die out" in a few years?), disco artists continue to enjoy much commercial success: Donna Summer is still recording in the traditional "disco" vein with 1989's "This Time I Know It's For Real."

One measure of disco's impact is the now-commonplace use and reliance upon synthesized (and programmed) drums, bass, and keyboards which began with the style at the end of the seventies (The brief craze for white suits and wide shirt collars, popularized in *Saturday Night Fever*, probably ended when the dry cleaning bills started coming in). Even jazz luminary Herbie Hancock jumped on the bandwagon with his strange video of moving maniquins in 1982.

And, while "new" bands like the Police, Men At Work, Eurythmics, the Pretenders, Culture Club, Duran Duran, and Human League populated the charts in 1983, right alongside were "new disco" hits as "Maniac," "She Works Hard For The Money," and "Twilight Zone."

Among the "new wave rock" bands, more than a few successfully wedded dance grooves to the chords and lyrical content of rock.

Since disco is a synthesis of rock, R & B, and funk styles, it would seem that the instruments' parts draw equally from these areas. The disco bass can be funky or bouncy, and should, as always, lock in with the rhythm of the bass drum. Typical disco drums feature a sixteenth-note pattern on the hi-hat, though sometimes eighth notes are used, featuring an alternatingly open and closed hi-hat. Here's what the four permutations of these two bass and two drum ideas might look like:

Example 108:

Example 109:

Example 110:

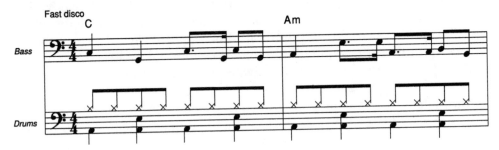

Example 111:

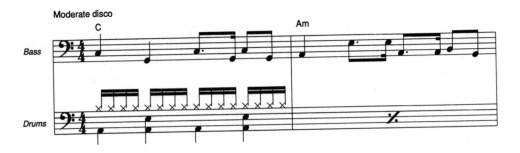

There are three main ways in which the guitar can contribute to the groove (certainly guitar lines and solos add to a piece, but here we speak of the guitar solely as a rhythm section instrument), by playing a constant, smooth chordal accompaniment in a sixteenth-note pattern:

Example 112:

by playing an accented, syncopated chordal "line":

Example 113:

or by playing a somewhat muted single-note repeating riff in rhythmic counterpoint with the rest of the rhythm players:

Example 114:

Of course, any of the above can be combined with the appropriate bass and
drums groove. Often the last approach, the "chicken" picking, is combined
with one of the previous stylings in a two-guitar rhythm section.

   This talk about "muted" riffs brings us to the role of the synthesizer in
disco-funk veins. You've all no doubt heard the cheesy sounds of European
disco music and its syrupy synth lines mimicking, usually, string sections
(violins, cellos, violas, and the like). "Grade-B" movie soundtracks seem to
favor this kind of tooth-rotting flavor, although scores to such "Grade-A"
movies as *Chariots of Fire* and *Midnight Express* show great style and artistry
in their use of synthesizers. Synthesizers are often used to recreate the sounds
of live string players in the studio, adding a smooth layer of "backing" to
the music —known as a "pad" among the proverbial pros. A second manner in which synths contribute is by playing a single-voice line, which can
be the "hook" to the song. Here's as example, which sounds something like
the main line in Rod Stewart's "Do Ya Think I'm Sexy?," a disco-inspired

variation of a rock tune:

Example 115:

Here the synth is, in a very direct sense, assuming the role which has traditionally been played by the lead guitar in rock.

A third thing the synthesizer can do is to simulate a funky bass riff, playing a part in the midrange or bass register. Stevie Wonder was one of the first well-known artists to incorporate this rhythmic approach into his music, first on clavinet, then on synth, as the technology improved. Just think of some of his many hits: "Higher Ground," "Superstitious," "Sir Duke," "You Ain't Done Nothin,'" and you get the picture! Once again, the success of this kind of part very much depends upon how well it meshes rhythmically with the rest of the musicians' parts to create an overall funky groove.

One last thought: if you consider yourself a "rocker," don't let the term "disco" scare you off into avoiding the applicability of dance grooves to your music. In today's creative climate of musical experimentation and blending of unexpected sounds and grooves, anything is possible.

Isn't that what the freedom of rock is supposed to be all about, anyway?

9

The Hard Rock Arrangement

"The spirit of rock stays alive..."

Just as R & B has hugely affected funk, mainstream rock has influenced its heavier, more aggressive, often darker stepchild, the style that is alternately known as heavy rock, hard rock, and heavy metal. There is another "heavy" subgenre we should consider here: punk rock and thrash music. This style is represented by bands like the Sex Pistols, Dead Kennedys, TSOL (True Sounds of Liberty), Husker Dü, Black Flag and Flipper—bands whose music retains the volume element of hard rock while playing it at convulsive speeds, often incorporating into their songs lyrical content of political nature (usually leftist).

Also drawing heavily upon mainstream rock while working with their own particular raisons d'etre are the areas of art rock, "new wave" (which is hardly new anymore), urban rock (with Lou Reed as a seminal practictioner) and "progressive" rock (the group Yes comes to mind) and numerous other sub-genres, most of which are truly experimental in nature. Because these areas account for such a great range of arranging styles, we will unfortunately not be able to cover them all in detail in this short book. However, the message which the great diversity of rock styles of arranging espouses is a clear one, one which is at the core of this discussion: the progression of rock arranging throughout the decades has followed some crazy kind of quiltwork pattern in which elements of one style are picked up by other groups who eventually may sprout their own "style." Witness 1989's hard rock/heavy metal group D.A.D., in which the sound and beat of metal meets dual fifties vintage Gretsch guitars, playing Duane Eddy-style rockabilly riffs in what is otherwise a straight-ahead modern hard rock context. And witness the release of Broadway composer genius Stephen Sondheim's "Losing My

Mind" (from his show *Follies*) as recorded by Liza Minnelli with a disco beat! Is this the sublime meeting the ridiculous, or is there about to be born a new crossover genre—something along the lines of Broadway disco?

Only time will tell. Through your own experimentation in rock arranging you may similarly create your own sounds or perhaps even your own style.

Some of the groups which bridged the gap from "rock" to "hard rock" were, first and foremost, Led Zeppelin, followed closely by Cream, the Jimi Hendrix Experience, the Who, Deep Purple, and Uriah Heep. Their hard-rocking sounds continued through the seventies with bands like Free, Grand Funk Railroad, the Sweet, Mott the Hoople, Queen, and Foreigner. Still present are the sounds of the pumping eighth-note bass and the 2 and 4 snare, along with the quintessential rock instrument—the electric guitar. But there are some subtle and some not-so-subtle differences to be heard.

Structurally, songs in this genre pretty much maintain the standard verse-chorus format. Some of the more "experimental" or "progressive" hard rock delves deeply into odd time signatures, with bands like Yes, Rush, and Genesis standing out as examples. But make no mistake about this: hard rock is, with few yet more and more frequent exceptions, 4/4 country.

"...under the assault of hi-tech"

There is a certain instantaneous reaction and immediate recognition when one hears hard rock. This feeling may be likened to that which one feels when trying to painstakingly copy a chord chart while one's neighbor enjoys, at maximum volume, the latest Metallica record. What is it that's so distinctive about this music?

It's been suggested that the hallmark of hard rock is the attitude with which it is played. For our purposes, the way in which hard rock is recorded is really the issue. When Mike Fink (Rolling Stone Ron Wood's drummer) was asked to talk about the differences between mainstream rock and hard rock, he mentioned these same two points: the difference in recording and the difference in playing, which follows the more aggressive attitude of hard rock. Fink mentions that the basic rhythm of the two styles is the same. Yet, in general, you will find rhythm section players actually playing —picking, popping, and hitting—harder on hard rock tunes than in other genres. This translates to a more powerful sound through the recording process. Some journeyman (and journeywoman) drummers lament the fact that in most metal, hard rock, punk, thrash, and even New Wave, their role is limited to that of timekeeper with little variation in rhythm and expression. Drummers do get to play with more freedom and dynamics when they are involved in a progressive rock or Art rock situation than when they are playing a simple, straight-ahead rock groove, but drums are only one element in the entire hard rock arrangement. Suffice it to say that the drummer's contribution to hard rock music is indeed to keep the time, provide simple accents and fills in appropriate places in the music, and, most importantly, to add excitement and propulsion by playing forcefully.

Here's an example of a particular drum beat which was used by two different drummers in two different situations:

Example 116:

If you are a drummer, you may recognize this as the "Charlie Watts" drumbeat. Charlie Watts, the Rolling Stones' drummer, has used this beat in countless rock and hard rock tunes. Its characteristic is the lack of cymbal or hi-hat hit on beats 2 and 4, which really brings the pop of the snare drum on those beats to the forefront. This same beat can be heard in the Traveling Wilburys' record "Handle With Care," yet there it is played in a much more relaxed, laid-back manner.

Contrast that song with, say, the Stones' "Start Me Up" or their "Mixed Emotions" and about the only similar thing you'll hear is—you guessed it—the drum beat.*

Before moving on, let's return to our talk about the actual recording of hard rock and discuss how the technology has influenced how we hear this music in its recorded form.

It is fair to say that there is not a great deal of variation in orchestration (instrumentation) within the area of hard rock. The majority of bands take their basic instrumentation from the power trio—guitar, bass, and drums with a vocalist who may be the fourth member—and may augment that combo to include a second guitar (a la Guns 'n' Roses, Def Leppard, and Aerosmith) and/or a keyboard/synth (like Bon Jovi, which has the two-guitar/synth lineup and Deep Purple, which had the one-guitar/synth lineup).

---

*Note: Charlie Watts does not play drums with the Wilburys.

What today's modern recording technology can do is make any size band to sound *GIGANTIC*, and it can do this for two reasons.

One, because of multitrack recording ("overdubbing" and "bouncing tracks"), many tracks of the same part can be recorded (which results in a very lush, thick texture) or many different tracks can be laid down to give the illusion of numerous musicians. Two, state-of-the-art consoles, mixers, microphones, and amplifiers can reproduce the high-wattage sounds of Marshall amps and loud drums more faithfully than was previously possible with more primitive electronic equipment. Listen to early power trios like Led Zeppelin, the Who, and the Jimi Hendrix Experience and you will hear multiple tracks, for sure, but if you then listen to a more contemporary power trio like Van Halen or Living Colour, you will hear that the instruments actually sound "bigger" by themselves, aside from overdubbing, and this phenomenon is due primarily to the modern recording studio's being, well, so modern.

As with any technological boom, recording technology has led to excesses and thus one often hears a commonly-voiced complaint about modern commercial rock arrangements: they are too busy and cluttered. Precisely because instruments can sound *HUGE*, one must exercise caution and restraint (remember our friend, Les S. Moore?) when faced with the possibility of adding numerous tracks to a simple, small combo arrangement, by either doubling an existing track or creating a new one.

The principle of economy should also be followed in the hard rock arrangement, as should the aspects of balance, focus, and variety.

Some hard rock music goes in for the "buzz saw" effect and the "gang" vocal approach, both which are pretty self-descriptive names. In terms of the perspective of a traditional arranger like Don Sebesky, an arrangement in which the tonal spectrum (we're talking about tonal balance here) does not vary much from the lead to the rhythm to the bass guitar would be an arrangement in need of arranging. But that would be like "arranging" the Beatles' music to fit the needs of, say, a Mantovani, wouldn't it? True, much hard rock leaves much to be desired in the traditional area of balance, but the music is what it is and should be accepted as such. There are bands whose arrangements do include multiple tracks of guitar spanning a broad tonal range, and to this author's ears, they are a far more interesting listen than the "buzz saw" bands. An example of the former is Guns 'n' Roses' "Welcome To The Jungle," with its dramatic opening of cascading guitars; an example of the latter might be a tune by Anthrax or Metallica, two hardcore metal bands which have gained a more widespread listening (and viewing on music video stations) public.

As we look at the arranging elements of economy, focus, and variety in relation to hard rock, we have to keep in mind that these concepts may or may not be relevant to the style, image, and level of sophistication of bands who espouse this rock style. Hard rock and metal are often stripped-down genres, relying mostly on bass, drums, and guitar for their distinctive sound. Out of Sebesky's four areas, the music of hard rock follows the principle of economy perhaps more than any other one. The hard rock combo's instrumentation is usually minimal, as mentioned above. Compare the orchestration of Elvis' "Viva Las Vegas" to the instrumentation in the Dead Kennedy's version. It just wouldn't sound right were the DK's to add layers of sound and instruments to their cover—it just wouldn't sound like the band.

The focus in the hard rock arrangement depends wholly on the instrumentation used in the piece. Since only the basic rock instruments are used, it is easier to maintain the primary and secondary focus throughout the hard rock tune. One's attention is generally focused primarily on either the lead guitar or the lead vocal, with the bass and drums providing the secondary focus in the arrangement, though they do get their solos from time to time. Indeed, one may postulate that the tremendous popularity of this genre among youth may be attributed to the fact that the music is "easy" to hear: simple instrumentation, simple rhythms, simple chords, simple (and repetitive) scales all make for uncomplicated listening.

Variety, which tends to go against economy, is not a distinguishing feature of most metal and hard rock. Variety in this style tends to be superimposed upon tunes, often by the addition of an acoustic guitar, gently picked or strummed as part of an introduction. The song which opens with an acoustic guitar, proceeds through a quiet first verse, and then rips into the heavy chords and tom-tom drum fills is clichéd by now. Sure, this kind of arrangement adds a dynamic element to the song, but in its most basic sense it is nothing particularly distinctive: start soft, get louder, then stay there.

By being aware of the elements of rock arranging which are often not developed in hard rock, it will be possible for you to create distinctive music in this style if you pay particular attention to these very elements. Hard rock does not have to be all midrange guitar and bass, all vocal and lead guitar, all dynamically static.

Rhythms

The basic feel of hard rock is the quarter note, which, accompanied by slow to moderate tempos, gives a heavy, ponderous sound to the music. The eighth note in the rhythm is about as complicated as this music usually gets, unless some elements of R & B or funk (a la Living Colour) are used. Following are a few measures of four grooves, which may sound to you like Def Leppard's "Pour A Little Sugar On Me," Free's "All Right Now," Joan Jett's "I Love Rock And Roll," and Led Zeppelin's "Good Times Bad Times."

Example 117:
"Sugar"

Example 118:
"All Right"

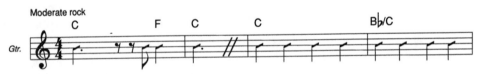

Example 119:
"Rock And Roll"

Example 120:
"Bad Times"

Note that the basic rhythm of each is pretty much the same. What is different is the chordal structure. Also be aware that hard rock employs mostly major chords and "power fifths" (a two-note chord comprised of only the root and fifth tones), with an occasional minor or dominant chord. Diminished and augmented tonalities are endangered species in this genre but they can be heard from time to time.

Now that we've discussed some of the features of hard rock, let's arrange a tune in that style. Imagine that you and your band has recently received an offer to record your first album on Strychnine Records. The record company wants a December release date to coincide with the winter holiday record buying season, and your producer suggests covering the perennial favorite "Silent Night." The things which you have to consider in working out an arrangement are those same aspects which we've been talking about all along: tempo and groove, key (we'll use the original melody and chords), form, dynamics, and orchestration.

The overall arranging concept has already been agreed upon— "Silent Night" as a heavy metal tune. We'll try to avoid most of the cliches associated with this genre and add some interest to our arrangement.

Deciding upon the groove also entails setting the tempo for the piece, as we've mentioned earlier. The time signature for "Silent Night" is 3/4, meaning that each measure contains three beats (the top number), and each one of those beats is a quarter note (the bottom number). In order to make the song "rock," we'll change the time signature to 4/4, and that new extra beat will, in effect, be inserted between the first and second beats of the 3/4 version, as follows:

Example 121:

The drummer in the band has come up with a heavy-duty beat that he thinks would be appropriate for the tune. Written out, it looks like this:

Example 122:

Note the quarter notes played on the hi-hat and snare. The bass-drum pattern shows more rhythmic variation, with a sixteenth-note rhythm on the third beat of each measure. This particular pattern is reminiscent of the rhythm of another Christmas favorite, "The Little Drummer Boy."

The tune will be played at a tempo equal to a metronome setting of about 60 (one beat clicking off about every second) which is a pretty slow tempo. However, this slow tempo is appropriate for two reasons: one, it fits the genre of the tune and two, it works with the overall concept, which is playing a sacred, religiously thematic tune ("Silent night, holy night,...all is calm...").

Now that the germ of the groove has been established by the drummer, let's turn our attention to the matter of key before we bring in the other instrumentalist(s). Before deciding upon a key, we should consider both the range of the tune's melody and the vocal range of the singer. The melody to "Silent Night" spans just over an octave—actually, an octave plus a note. The vocalist in our fictitious band has a very wide range, and his top note (the highest note he can hit on a good day) is the B two octaves above middle C. He wants to utilize his upper vocal limit in this tune, and, as a matter of fact, the highest note in "Silent Night" occurs on the lyric "heavenly" (as in "heavenly sleep").* When taken together, the vocalist's range plus the parameters of hard rock—power chords using the open strings of guitar when possible—suggest that this version be played in the key of E major, the "key of the ancient Aztecs," as one particularly cynical observer has suggested. This key will allow the guitarist to use the open E and A strings, which sustain longer than unfretted (unstopped) strings. Also, the vocalist can go almost as high as his top note when he sings the A two octaves above middle C for "heavenly." In E major, the range of the melody looks like this:

Example 123:

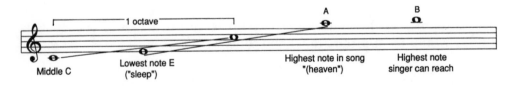

Middle C   Lowest note E   Highest note in song   Highest note
             ("sleep")   "(heaven)"   singer can reach

---

*It is more than coincidence that the word "heaven," which has lofty and "high" connotations, is the high note in the song. This is an excellent example of how songwriters can express an emotion by tying a particular note to a particular word.

The bassist's part comes next, and it looks like this:

Example 124:

It's simple, to the point, and moreover, does not follow the bass-drum pattern on the third beat. This would be "too much" for the straightforward, hard rock concept of the piece. Were the bassist to play the same figure as the drummer, it would detract from the little drummer boy's syncopation, rather than complement it. The rhythm guitar part, however, will mimic this figure, but on the first beat of each measure. In essence, then, the guitarist is the first to play this figure which is "answered" by the drummer's bass drum on beat three.

Regarding the orchestration of the tune, the band and its producer (who is also wearing the hat of arranger in this situation) would like to hear a very raw, stripped-down version of "Silent Night." They decide that the song will be recorded "live," with just bass, drums, guitar and a "scratch" or reference vocal. The producer/arranger then hits upon adding an instrument somewhat traditionally associated with Christmas to the production: bells. Bells (or the chime-like glockenspiel) have a very delicate sound, and this contrasts nicely with the "heavy" sounding rhythm section. The bells, it has been decided, will be played by an outside musician brought to augment the three-piece combo, who will play them on an intro section and in a solo section. Remember, polar opposites (fast-slow, metal-bluegrass, etc.) often can work wonders for an arrangement. It behooves the arranger not to discard any strange ideas just because they at first appear antithetical to the preconceived notion of the song.

In this case, the producer/arranger has admirably earned his points—his salary. Now the orchestration is set, and we're beginning to get an idea of the form, the structure of the tune. "Silent Night" happens to be a song which only has one section, which is 24 measures long. If recorded this way, the song would be far too short for a record, so the vocalist suggests writing (sacrilege!) a second section, with a new lyric following the original melody. Then, the song could be recorded with the following form: intro, verse, solo section, verse, outro (like an intro, but occurring at the end of a song). All agree, until they see what the vocalist has penned:

Baby, you're tight; holy and right.
Warm and nice, smelling like spice.
Ride our rocket and blast to the moon
We will fly through the whole afternoon.
Love like ours runs so deep.
We'll sleep in heavenly sleep.

Hmm. You can almost see the choir of angels tapping their feet, flapping their wings, and raising their fists to this one.

So as not to have this potential number-one hit song blasted and boycotted by the PMRC, the band's producer not so subtly directs some lyric changes, eliminating the obvious sexual references, which appear in almost every line of the lyric. A new verse is written and accepted by all. It's more in line with the holiday spirit and contains no references to rockets, or blasting to the moon.

Silent night, feeling all right,
Cool down, Pops, don't be up tight.
I won't do nothing to mess up your scene.
I'll fix the muffler on my killer machine.
I'll sing to your shining star.
The cruise control's set on my car.

The dynamics of the cover version, which the band will very cleverly call "Sylint Nyyte," will not follow the "loud-louder-louder" still formula. Instead, the song will open forcefully ("ff" or fortissimo in the lingo of dynamic markings), come down in volume somewhat during the first verse ("f" or forte), get louder during the glockenspiel solo, get softer during the second verse and stay at that level throughout the outro. The various players should, therefore, adjust their playing volumes accordingly.

Now everyone knows how to play their parts, but once the song is run through, the producer/arranger as well as the band members pick up on the fact that the instrumental parts don't change at all as the song proceeds through the various verse sections and solo sections. The guitarist suggests that during the intro, solo, and outro sections, the band gets a little more driving. They accomplish this by having the drummer play eighth notes on the hi-hat while the guitarist plays an eighth-note rhythm.

This turns out to work just fine, and the basic arrangement for "Sylint Nyyte" is now set.

And the rest, as they say, is rock history . . .

Arranging in a hard-rock style can be just as experimental and creative as are those involved in the project. In fact, precisely because much metal and hard rock sounds as if it were all cut from the same mold, this area offers much to the fledgling arranger. As we have shown, the principles of a good arrangement can remain in effect from one genre to another. It is up to you to bring your special talents and skills to whatever area of rock you choose to arrange.

10

The Folk Arrangement

"There are no bridges in folk songs because the peasants died building them."
—*Eugene Chadbourne*

There is no easy definition for folk music. Specialists in the field have been known to come to blows over the meaning of the phrase. The safe way out—and the one we take here—is to think of the folk style primarily as a sound which places emphasis on the meaning of the lyrics. But it is a sound (or collection of sounds) that is immediately identifiable with particular groups of people and particular places. There can be no doubt, for example, where the Gypsy Kings are from, just as the Cajun music, currently enjoying such wide popularity with its wild energy and occasional French lyrics, is readily identifiable as coming from the Bayou in the southeastern United States. Paul Simon drew upon the music of southern Africa for his highly acclaimed *Graceland* album, while Peter Gabriel has drawn a great deal of influence from northern Africa and India. Brazilian music, with its sophisticated rhythms and harmonies, has been another folk style that has occasionally worked its way into the mainstream. Ever since the early sixties, these and other native styles have had their impact on rock, just as rock has had its impact on them. Perhaps the best known of these musics are the blues and country music, which we have discussed elsewhere. But given the current "everything goes" climate in the rock scene today and the surprising hits from the likes of Tracy Chapman and Suzanne Vega over the past few years, it probably is a good idea to include a few words on the distinctive elements of folk styles and how they can be included in the overall framework of rock.

Oddly, like techno-rock, with its banks of synths and drum machines, much of the contemporary folk sound is itself a product of high technology. Back in the bad old days, when folkies did nothing but protest, they were playing big acoustic guitars through—gulp!—microphones. While this was perfectly alright in the recording studio (after all, the Beatles were using the acoustic as a primary rhythm instrument in 1964 and 1965), it was extremely dangerous to attempt to play acoustic guitars at big concert settings where the mike could feedback and give the soundman bad dreams for nights on end.

But in the mid-seventies, several savvy instrument makers began to build special pickups into acoustic guitars that would preserve their special sound and yet also allow them to be played live with synths, electrics, even bass and drums. These pickups are built into the saddle of the bridge and draw upon the vibration of the guitar top rather than on the electromagnetic interaction between the metal string and the coils. Where the folk style is musically distinctive, then, is in its instrumentation and the way in which those instruments are used. Along with the acoustic guitar, which often serves as the focus of the instrumental arrangement, we also find fiddles (as opposed to violins), a variety of bluegrass instruments (especially the banjo and the mandolin), as well as various ethnic instruments, ranging from the accordion (transplanted from continental Europe and essential to the cajun sound) and the celtic harp to the tabla (a double drum from India), the host of percussion instruments favored in northern Africa, and the Caribbean steel drum.

But folk music is more than ethnic sounds to the contemporary American mind. For many of us, folk is Bob Dylan singing like a chain saw to guitar accompaniment, or else it is the tight arrangements and exquisite fingerpicking of James Taylor. It can also be the clear, open harmonies of Peter, Paul, and Mary or the wicked irony of Leonard Cohen. Still others these days base their definition of folk music on lyrical content—songs that are extremely topical or that tell a story are generally pretty easy to classify as folk songs.

So, it might be easier to say what folk music isn't: it can be simple music with simple structure (witness the quote opening up this chapter), but it can also be made up of extremely complicated rhythmic, harmonic, and melodic patterns (Brazilian and Indian musics sound very sophisticated to western ears). In other words, about the only sure thing you can say about folk music is that it isn't easy to define.

Still, even though we can't say what exactly it is, we often know folk music when we hear it—a bit like the Supreme Court talking about pornography.

Consider Peter Gabriel, one of the most versatile performers and song-writers on the scene today. On his album, *Passion*, comprised of music written for Martin Scorcese's film, *The Last Temptation of Christ*, Gabriel on the last track, "Bread And Wine," sets a penny whistle over a richly textured synthesizer background. The effect calls to mind traditional Irish music—a beautiful, sad ballad—but the dressing itself is very modern. The melody resembles very much the excerpt cited here:

Example 125:

The secret of the arrangement, however, is the absence of attack (for "attack," see the Appendix) in the synthesizer accompaniment. The simple harmonies, which change every two beats, blend from one to the next.

The tune is composed in two parts. The first is a short four-measure phrase that is repeated. The second part features contrasting material that leads eventually to the tonic. The result is a verse form in the typical Irish ballad style. Only when the synth, with added texture from the electric double violin, has gone through this verse twice does the penny whistle enter as the solo instrument. There is no bridge in the piece. In sharp contrast to this is the opening cut on the album, "The Feeling Begins," which features a percussion section composed of octabans, surdus, skins, and shakers. Beneath the introduction, an Armenian melody called "The Wind Subsides" (played on the violin and the Armenian doudouk), Gabriel gradually builds a massive rhythm, based on a dance from the same region, which eventually overruns the mournful tune.

Is this rock? Perhaps; perhaps not; perhaps it is too early to say. The point here is that folk music—in this case, from Armenia—often provides a base on which to experiment and develop new sounds from which the rock of the future can be derived. This is somewhat like what George Harrison was doing in his work with the Beatles back in 1966, when he began studying Indian music seriously. The result of such efforts can be heard in the guitar solo from "Taxman" on the *Revolver* album as well as the guitar solo on "Good Morning Good Morning" on *Sgt. Pepper's*. In both cases, the guitar technique used came from Harrison's sitar playing, with the pulled-off notes having as much attack as the picked notes.

If these examples seem too far out for many people, there are many instances in which a "folk" sound has served as the basis for a rock song. The arrangement of Suzanne Vega's song "Luka" is built around a deceptively simple guitar part played on the acoustic. Couched among a synth track, an electric guitar, bass, and drums, the acoustic provides the rhythmic motifs that the other instruments follow.

Vega's style as a player is very interesting. For several years, she toured around as a solo performer, and bootleg tapes from that time show that in her performances, she rarely played full chords in her songs, except when she approached the chorus. Instead, she accompanied her vocal melodies with rather syncopated guitar parts on the middle reaches of the neck, generally played on the top four strings. This was the case with "Luka."

In the recording of the song from her second album, the other instruments are responding to what is going on on the acoustic. After the solo acoustic opening, which is also the accompaniment to the verse, the synth responds with a series of complementary, open triads set against the guitar turnaround at the end of the lyric line. Only when the acoustic guitar and the synth come to the chorus does the rest of the band enter.

There are other signs of the folk influence here, most notably in the mixing. For example, given the importance of the lyric, the vocal is obviously going to be up front. And then there is the quality of the vocal. We don't mean "good" or "bad" but rather, the strength of the voice. Vega is no belter—Pat Benatar would have little trouble blowing Vega offstage in a volume contest. But she does make her presence felt by the way in which she enunciates the words—something that is evident, again, in the mix, which creates a space around the voice. As the case of Bob Dylan shows, the folk singer doesn't necessarily have to have a beautiful voice. And as Vega shows, the folk singer doesn't even have to have the capacity to sing loudly. It comes down to a matter of what they call "delivery"—how they convey the meaning of the words through the way in which they deliver a line.

Using Folk Instrumentation and Style

We have already mentioned some of the exotic instruments currently being used on rock recordings that betray the folk influence—George Harrison's introduction of the sitar to young Western audiences in the sixties, Peter Gabriel's use of North African drums, and so on. Using the instruments is not enough: what really identifies their "folk" nature is how they're played. For example, when is a violin not a violin? When it's played like a fiddle.

This isn't just one of those corny riddles you can sometimes hear among classical musicians (something along the lines of the joke about how one gets to Carnegie Hall—practice). Different musical styles foster different playing techniques. For example, there is fingerpicking—Kansas's lugubrious hit "Dust In The Wind"—and then there's fingerpicking—Guy Van Duser playing the John Phillip Sousa march "Stars And Stripes Forever" (including piccolo parts) on the guitar.

James Taylor is an example of a folk musician who has combined elements of folk and rock to create a distinctive sound. A terrific fingerstyle guitarist, Taylor writes extremely melodic material over tightly arranged chords. Using this as the basis of his arrangement, he then uses instrumental combinations that, in another time, would have been impossible to imagine—a case in point is blending the acoustic with keyboards, electric guitar, bass, drums, and back-up vocalists in "Never Die Young." The acoustic guitar, processed with digital delay and doubled by the synth, opens the song. After running twice through the introductory line (based on the accompaniment to the opening half of the verse), Taylor brings in the second half of the introduction, and with it comes the electric, playing light, complementary rhythmic fills. The synth, for its part, then plays only on the downbeat. The overall structure of the song looks like this:

Intro	*Intro (first half, transition)*
Verse	*Solo (bridge)*
Verse	*Verse*
Bridge	*Verse*
Verse	*Verse*
Verse	*Intro*
Fade	

The introduction comes in two parts, which Taylor plays with to great effect. Depending on the placement in the song, the first part can be either the introduction itself, the first half of the verse, or the transition to the solo. The fade is based on the second half of the introduction. All in all, what Taylor does is follow Nelson Riddle's ideas cited at the beginning of the book—derive material from the verse for the introduction to create a greater sense of the whole. As Taylor shows, this is as viable for "folk" as it is for any other style of popular music.

If folk conveys an entire range of different sounds, we can still find certain common elements in songs written and performed by players coming out of the folk scene. Like Vega's "Luka," it is the acoustic that sets the pace and the rhythm of "Never Die Young." Similarly, it is the acoustic that provides the groundwork for all of the various portions of the song.

If you are looking to follow a folk sound, then put the acoustic guitar way up front in the mix, right behind the vocal. And though the structure of Taylor's song looks convoluted, it really involves only three different verse-length fragments, two of which are related.

In other words—and as we have said before—keep the structure of your folk arrangement simple. By using different rhythmic patterns in the various sections, you can create a wide range of sounds that will always provoke the interest of your audience.

Lastly, if you have a yen for a tabla drum, don't necessarily expect your kit drummer to be able to do it. The rhythm patterns that sound great on a kit sound a little sad on the tabla. The reverse holds true as well: the drum kit isn't an ideal vehicle for conveying Indian rhythms, either. Ethnic instruments such as the tabla evolved in keeping with their respective musical traditions. Trying to use them in another style generally does not work. Ask yourself whether it is the sound of the instrument you want or its particular capabilities as a rhythmic, melodic, or harmonic fixture.

Above all else, when you begin exploring folk and ethnic sounds, ask yourself what kind of texture you are looking for. If it is a certain kind of rhythm, don't overload the arrangement with harmonic accompaniment that will drown out your rhythm section. As always, if you keep the focus on one thing, the chances are that the listener will be able to hear what you want him or her to hear.

PART III
Dressing in Style

11

MIDI and the Arranger

by Ken Hamberg

Setting the Scene

The guitarist in your band invites you to attend a recording session he's playing. He's very excited and he thinks you'll get a kick out of it; he tells you the studio has 64 tracks of recording, automation, lots of outboard gear, and all he has to bring is his guitar. They supply everything else. You can see it all in your mind's eye: a huge room with a ceiling twenty feet high, hi-tech recessed lighting, black and chrome everywhere. Amplifiers stacked against the wall, a board big enough to keep the Fail Safe boys deep in the mountains of Colorado pretty happy, and a forest of the best microphones anywhere. And to top it all off, you imagine a huge tape machine with tape two inches wide ripping around above the federal speed limit capturing the hottest, fattest sound on the planet.

But as you approach the building, you are perplexed. The guitarist must have gotten the address confused, because you're in a residential area and what he described to you sounded as if it were industrial strength. Have faith, you tell yourself, as you press the doorbell. A character who looks like a mad scientist—at least he looks likes an engineer—opens the door and you find yourself in somebody's *house*. Something is very wrong here, you think, as he leads you down into the basement.

Then it gets even weirder. You see the washing machine, and you see some movable fiberboard barriers; you see the bare light bulbs. But what you're hearing an absolutely incredible sound you think it's a big brass band or something but it sounds a lot cleaner than that—coming out of a pair of very serious speakers set around an object that looks awfully like a computer. The guy who answered the door has taken a seat between the speakers and is moving a free hand around the table top like a Ouija player.

Bewildered, you focus on the music: the rich blare of tightly executed horn blasts, thundering drums, and velvety synthesizer textures supported by a crisp, punchy bass line. You can hear all the elements in the arrangement very distinctly. But it doesn't jibe with what you see. You don't see a seventeen-piece big band set up the furnace. You don't see a single drum lying next to the gardening tools. And when you look closer, you realize that you don't even see a big, whopping tape machine. The only moving part in the entire basement is the guy's hand. Your friend isn't here yet. And now that strange-looking guy is talking to himself—"If I stretch this note out here and make this one shorter, and goose the bass here, that should do it." His hand starts flying around the table top.

The music suddenly stops, and all you hear is a light clicking sound. Then it starts up again, the same piece, only it's different. The chord on the downbeat now lasts into the next beat, while the bass has all the whammy of an earthquake. But the guy didn't move any dials; he didn't rewind the tape; then again, he didn't have any tape to rewind.

What's going on here? Is this one of those flashbacks your dad always warned you about? Maybe it's the Twilight Zone. Oh, no, it can't be that. This sounds too good.

Welcome to the wonderful world of MIDI. . .

Technology Is Our Friend

MIDI is an acronym for *Musical Instrument Digital Interface,* and what we've been seeing here is a demonstration of how the computer has revolutionized life in the world of music, by taking sounds generated by a group of synthesizers and bringing them all together into an ensemble that can be played by a single individual. This isn't the one-man band; it's the one-man symphony orchestra, and the range of sounds he's got to work with is immeasurably more varied than the Oshkosh State Philharmonic.

In this chapter, we are going to look a bit at synthesizers, how MIDI works, and what you'll need to get started. In the main, though, we are going to discuss how MIDI can work for you when the time comes to arrange your music. No, not just arrange: because MIDI works with the instruments themselves, as well as with any compatible machinery you might want to include (such as a recorder), it is also becoming a big part of actual onstage performance. In that sense, MIDI is the biggest thing to hit music since the Industrial Revolution.

Indeed, though some people may find this a little hard to swallow, MIDI has completely altered the entire craft and art of making music. Back in the bad old days (1977, say), composing, arranging, and performing were three separate stages in the process of making music. First, you wrote the piece; then you arranged it. Finally, you or someone else would perform it. Would the performance be exactly as you imagined it? Maybe the drummer had a big fight with his girlfriend; maybe the guitarist pierced the tip of his middle finger with the end of a guitar string.

MIDI has changed all that: in a way, it is rather like composing classical-style, where composition involves arranging as well. But even there, there is still that gap between the arrangement and the performance. With MIDI, you can compose, arrange, and create the performance all at the same time. What is more, because MIDI involves computers and one of the two basic functions of the computer is to remember things, you can store that very same performance away on a diskette and play it back whenever you want. And because the other basic function of the computer is that it allows you to process the things it remembers, you can alter any aspect of the performance whenever you feel like it.

So what does that mean? Well, for one thing, it means that if you're getting ready to go into the studio, you can arrange your song exactly the way you want it and have something tangible to play for the various members of your band when it comes time to teach them their parts—you can do this with music notation as well, but not that many people read music nowadays beyond the rough chord chart or the single-line melody (taken at a very slow tempo, thank you very much).

Or it means that you can tell the rest of the band to take a hike, that you, like Lawrence of Arabia, will beat the Turks on your own—you, that is, armed with only your computer and your trusty bank of synths. You already have the parts you want and you already have the sounds that you want. Who needs a bunch of morons who have the sense of time of a centipede and the tuning ear of an aardvark?

But you wouldn't do such a thing to your buddies, now would you?

As we move into the nineties, the either/or questions that raised their ugly heads when first synths, then computers, made their way onto the scene —should I use only live musicians or should I use only synths?—have gradually given way to a healthy mix between the two, in which the performer will use both natural instruments and synthesizers.

Either way, MIDI can be a terrific tool. But first you have to get a sense of how it works. What's in it for you as a rock arranger/composer? As we'll discover, the possibilities are endless. Let's see what it can do and what you can do with it. But first we have to know what it is.

The Music Instrument Digital Interface is basically what they call a protocol, an agreement between manufacturers of electronic musical instruments that allows a single player to play many keyboards at the same time from a single keyboard. MIDI reduces all kinds of musical events to simple zeros and ones. Anything from where a note is played, to how loud it is played, to how long it lasts is communicated in a serial data stream from one keyboard instrument to another. This information is transmitted at roughly 1/30 of a millisecond—which is a little faster than the flap of a hummingbird's wing.

Yeah? So what does that mean? To understand that, you have to understand what synthesizers were like before MIDI. Back in ancient times, a synth player who wanted to layer or enhance his sound (orchestrate) was limited to using the products of one manufacturer alone. The reason for this was a signaling process called control voltage which assigned a certain amount of voltage to a given pitch. Since there was no standardization of control voltage among the instrument manufacturers, each had his own system to make it happen. To make matters worse, the early synths were capable of rendering only one sound at a time. The result of all this was that if you wanted to play a chord or create certain textures, you had to buy two or three of everything.

Thus, you ended up with the Keith Emerson music store effect—where the stage looked like a floor display of a music store. Guys like this were not very popular with the road crew. Before MIDI, players needed masses of equipment to create the kind of big sound synthesizers had the potential of offering—the kind of sound we just naturally expect today from just a few keyboards and a few rack mounted synthesizers.

The next step came with programmable synths. In the old days sounds were created manually, by twiddling knobs and levers and using patch cords to connect the various sound generators, which explains why we use the common term patch to describe any sound program. You could only save your information on file cards. Things could get pretty complicated on stage if you wanted to change sounds during a song and couldn't read the file card because of the light show going on around you. Programmable synths solved this problem by placing a little memory chip inside the synthesizer. Now all that knob-twiddling done to create the ultimate imitation Hammond organ or jet plane taking off could be saved and played over and over.

What is more, the nature of the sounds produced by synthesizers has changed rather dramatically over the years. To get a sense of what early synthesized tones were like, check out the theme to the television show, *Dr. Who*. There, the entire score was created in an electronic music lab. It probably helped that the program was (and is, though the theme was composed and recorded back in 1965) science fiction. The rattling vibrations and hums made by the frequency modulators and God knows what else somehow managed to create the groove of the piece. It sounds musical, but it could never be confused with the love theme from *Dr. Zhivago*: these were clearly sounds produced by machines that even Dr. Frankenstein would have admired.

The first synths were admired for, well, their synthesized sound. Walter (later Wendy) Carlos broke into the charts in the late sixties with *Switched On Bach*, an all-synthesizer rendition of several mainstays from the Bach repertoire. It had nothing to do with the quality of the performances; rather, it was the notion that it could be done at all. The more envelope, the more happy. By the late seventies, though, the Mellotron provided rock musicians with the first genuine copy of a fake string section. And as the Rhythm Ace, with "cymbals" that sounded like spit in a hot frying pan, gradually gave way to the drum machine, which sounded like robots from Andromeda, the technologists were learning how to record natural sounds on little bits of silicon.

Enter sampling—and the synth no longer depended on sounding simply weird. The button that said "strings" was actually using the sounds of strings and making them playable on a keyboard. And when you heard that hot banjo lick on a record—was that really a banjo?

MIDI was a sort of logical step in all of this, though that's a bit like saying the space shuttle is a logical development of the Wright Brothers' airplane: one can fly you a few hundred yards down a North Carolina beach; the other can take you to the moon. MIDI enhances the programmability of a huge assort ment of synthesizer generated sounds, both natural (i.e., sampled) and synthesized, to give the composer/arranger/performer the kind of tonal palette that was unimaginable even fifteen years ago.

Sequencing

But as we learned when we looked at the sample of the full score back in the chapter on musical rudiments, music isn't just pitches and timbres, chords and sonorities. Music is also a matter of *time*—time in terms of rhythm, time in terms of meter. MIDI addresses this issue as well, because an essential element in all of the musical software programs is the perfection of the computer's time keeping.

Keeping good time is one of the toughest aspects of the musician's work; indeed, many classical musicians practice hours upon hours not just to get the notes right, but to get them in rhythm as well. A sluggish day, and your timing can be off. You miss your entrances; you're just a bit late. Even if you're working from beautifully copied charts, the rhythm copied out on the page is not necessarily going to be what you actually play.

Quantization, one of MIDI's more charming applications, is the way out of this problem. It is, in short, a means of improving or perfecting your time. What it does is take your performance and adjust it to the lowest note value of that passage. For instance, lets say you play a difficult sixteenth-note run a little clumsily. All the notes are right, but your timing is off. Quantization will adjust the attacks of each note to the nearest sixteenth value and you'll sound bang on the beat.

Lets's take another example of correcting your playing from the opposite point of view. You play a difficult passage with correct timing but your dynamic is very inconsistent. Some notes sound too loud, some too soft. Through an adjustment in velocity, which is a MIDI term describing loudness and softness of attack (louder notes are hit faster and harder), you can edit the notes either individually or as a group to achieve a more consistent and realistic sound. The whole edit takes seconds.

Ten points for the computer age in music.

But as you begin to experiment with MIDI, you will find that your work as an arranger will involve many of the same issues discussed elsewhere in this book. The technology may be different, but the proverbial song remains the same. MIDI, at least at the present time, hasn't altered musical style per se.

What it *has* changed in terms of the music is the kind of questions you ask yourself as you arrange a piece. As before, depending on the style in which you're working, you need to think about orchestration. In the good old, bad old days, you chose an instrument for its particular sound. Any number of instruments, for example, can fill in the bass—acoustic or electric bass, tuba, bass saxophone, bassoon. With MIDI, you can choose either an instrument or a sound.

Here's a typical arranger's idea: "I want something that sounds like a breathy flute, but I also want it to have the edge of an oboe and a lot of decay." Old solution: Get a flute player with asthma and an oboist, make sure they're in tune, record the two separate tracks, and run them both through a lot of reverb. In the mix, place them in the same location in stereo space and twiddle with knobs for a little while until you can't tell which instrument is which and call it a day.

You get the picture: MIDI allows you to slave synthesizers together so that you can blend different sounds. The only thing you need to be sure of is that at least one of the synths has a keyboard. But to take full advantage of what MIDI can do for you, you need to have a computer. And so MIDI, which is really nothing more than a means of turning a bunch of synthesizers into an ensemble in which the various instruments can "talk" to each other, becomes the killer time and orchestration machine.

Sequencers are the software programs written for a variety of computers that allow you to record and edit music through MIDI. They all attempt to simulate the recording operation of a real tape machine. They all have features like play, record, rewind, and punch-in so the whole process is pretty easily related to more conventional recording techniques. If you have ever used or owned a home four-track cassette recorder, you'll take to the process right away. Most of the better programs try to create an easy and friendly environment to work in, and after a while you forget that you are using a computer. It can really be a fast, fun way to work. Tracks are laid out in order very much like a track sheet is in the recording studio. This allows you to name and describe the information on each track. In many sequencers you actually press play and record (on some, simply R for record) to begin recording. So that's kept pretty simple and identifiable as well.

And that is only one aspect of your average sequencing program, because what sequencing basically does is allow you to use your computer as a recording studio into which you store all the information you need to drive your synthesizers through a piece. That's why the guy with the slightly demonic, faraway look in his eyes who answered the door didn't have a tape recorder in his basement: he didn't need one. He had recorded all of the material on his computer by means of his sequencing program.

Here's a typical way in which you might use a sequencing program, using your computer as a recording studio. You might assign your drum part to MIDI Channel 1 on Track 1 of the sequencer (the computer), MIDI Channel 2 to Track 2 for the bass line, and so on. As in a recording studio, each sound is assigned its own channel and track, and each musical part is assigned an appropriate sound.

Let's assume you've got your keyboard and drum machine cranked up and you are ready to write your big hit. Your first instrument is actually guitar or maybe the saxophone or drums and you might have some anxiety about your keyboard playing ability. Imagine that you're a guitarist, for instance. You can now play your synthesizers from your guitar—just like Adrian

Belew. MIDI "retrofits" are available for everyone and are easy to install. It's not just for keyboard players anymore. MIDI now offers controller capabilities to just about every instrument imaginable from an accordion to a trumpet.

In addition to the considerable ease with which any player can access MIDI—regardless of his or her instrument or whether he or she has reached the age of consent—there is a new and rather fundamental idea in MIDI that you are playing a sound as opposed to an instrument. When we first learn to play the instrument we choose to study, we are taught various techniques that enable us to produce the sounds best known to that instrument. We use those techniques to make that instrument sound best and most familiar to our audience, be it a flute or piano or cello. We also understand that the sounds that we can produce from that instrument are specific to that instrument and also limited by the capabilities and construction of that instrument (assuming we're not using a lot of electronic toys to change its sound). We don't normally expect to be able to bend notes on a piano the way we can on a guitar, for instance, nor should we expect to execute a barrelhouse piano one-finger glissando on a trombone.

The MIDI sound palette contains just about every instrument available (plus some hybrid sounds that don't really exist). To a certain extent this is very democratic, since everybody's natural technique sort of goes out the window. We all have to listen more intently to the instruments we hear all the time in order to faithfully reproduce their sound from a performance aspect.

Because as a MIDI musician you are playing sounds, simulations or recordings of real instruments—not the real instruments themselves. What results is an exciting new discipline—a new technique that you might call playing the sound. The better you get at it, the more you sound like the private orchestra of your dreams, with you as player/arranger/conductor. The point is this: play the sound! Don't worry about your keyboard chops because there are a lot of sounds at your disposal that don't play well with keyboard technique. Believe me, you'll know them when you hear them. The MIDI musician has to learn to think like a variety of instrumentalists to get the musical point across. The keyboard or whatever controller you use is just a tool; it's only part of the composing process—a sort of digital typewriter that lets you get your ideas onto disk. Traditional technique is not quite the factor in this recording process. You have the flexibility of playing a tremendous variety of instrument sounds and mimicking those instruments convincingly. You also have the ability to take those sounds to new musical places and create textures and arrangements that are not possible in the "real" musical world. Things can get real interesting out there on the cutting edge. Your ears and imagination define the boundaries.

One of the great things about working in a tapeless environment is that you can speed up or slow down the music without changing the pitch. So you can play a more difficult passage exactly the way you want it to sound at a slower tempo, record it, and then play it back at the actual tempo of the song without ever changing key or transposing. Tape won't do that for you. With tape you're changing the speed of the motor and therefore the pitch. With MIDI you're just changing the tempo. Big difference.

You might find that after you finish your song to your satisfaction that your singer can't cut it in that key. No problem. You simply transpose it up or down until you find the key in which he or she sounds best and then save it. Maybe you think the song is a little too fast. You can play it back instantly at a number of tempos and choose the one you want or save a selection of tempos if you can't decide.

But say that you don't have the appropriate hardware to make your guitar, for example, synthesizer-capable. MIDI makes the keyboard accessible to a musically-minded character who is all thumbs and no fingers. In conventional tape recording, you have to re-record a good performance that is marred by just a couple of wrong notes. This usually involves the risky process called punching in—where one false punch could ruin the track entirely. In sequence recording, you can simply search out the wrong notes and either delete them or substitute them in seconds. You can copy entire sections of a song if they repeat, and if you feel the performance and sound is what you want to hear, you won't have to re-record them.

The same applies to ostinatos and other repetitious musical material. In short, you can save a lot of time. And though MIDI enables you to slave synthesizers together, you can treat each voice individually. You can separate sounds on the same track through the split-and-merge feature. Splitting will enable you to take, for instance, a track having a bass drum and snare sound on it and remove the snare entirely and relocate it to another track on the sequencer. This is very helpful if you wanted to use several different snare sounds in the same song to create the ultimate snare drum. The merge feature is analogous to composite tracks in conventional recording. You could record four or ten different versions of the same solo, pick the sections you like and merge them together onto a single track for easy reference and mixing. The possibilities are endless, literally.

MIDI currently transmits on 16 separate MIDI channels (soon to be 32). It's a great means of keeping your sounds separate and, more crucially, of keeping information separate. With MIDI channelizing, a drum part will not play a horn sound, or a flute solo won't be doubled by an electric bass sound (unless you want it to). You assign a MIDI channel to a track on a sequencer and you have the same separation you'd have on a professional 24-track recorder.

So, MIDI allows you to compose and play all the parts yourself. There is nothing particularly new about this in rock and pop music. In the 1950s the guitarist Les Paul invented and experimented with an eight-track tape recorder, layering performances he himself had played. Artists as diverse as Stevie Wonder, Paul McCartney, Prince, Todd Rundgren, and Steve Winwood have all released records on which they played all the instruments themselves.

However, all these recordings required thousands of dollars of both instrument and recording equipment as well as some sort of professional recording facility—and, to add to the bill, an engineer. You can potentially make music that sounds just as good if not qualitatively better than some of these recordings in your own home. Through MIDI you can enjoy the same degree of self-containment and control over your composition and performance that these artists have enjoyed at a fraction of the cost in both equipment and studio time.

So, with nothing but a synthesizer, a computer, and some software, you can have a home recording studio that deals in the same measure of sound as the most expensive professional studio in the world.

MIDI and the Arranger

Manipulating sounds (orchestrating) and rhythms: these are two topics we've talked about a great deal in this book. And as we have seen, this is exactly what MIDI has to offer, only instead of doing it on paper or through negotiations with your fellow musicians, you're doing it yourself with real sound.

But for all the perfection it has to offer—the perfect timing, the perfect tuning, the perfect digital sound—you still have to make many of the same choices as before. What MIDI does do for your arranging is take some of the trial out of the error. You don't have to wait until the next rehearsal to see how the new B section in your song will sound. Will the bass part you've charted really go with those chords? Is the rhythm section really as locked in as you imagine, or does it just look good on paper? MIDI allows you to check these out and experiment with them *before* you make those first fateful steps into the studio.

That having been said, MIDI can put you in a musical minefield, simply because of its power and versatility. Alexander Pope said that a little knowledge is a dangerous thing; that can hold true for imagination as well. What if you had some Hindu goddess with eight arms and four legs sitting in as your drummer, and she had Steve Gadd's chops in every one of those arms and a quadruple bass drum set as well as a hi-hat (which she'd presumably play with one of her three noses)?

Kind of interesting. But more than a little weird, as well. Quite apart from sounding a bit like an orchestrated avalanche, it's a bit difficult imagining any of the styles we've discussed here making much sense amidst all of that percussive turmoil. As a player-arranger working up a drum track on MIDI, you need to think like a drummer if you want it to sound realistic. Dream of Siva, by all means, but think of one normal person with four limbs playing a drum kit. You may have 850 different drum and percussion sounds in your collection of samples, but that doesn't mean you have to use each and every one of them every time you boot up your sequencer.

Or say you have some terrific sounds in your sample collection—a murmuring brook, a girl screaming to high heaven, and a sample of a helicopter lifting off that you got straight from the R&D boys at Sikorsky Aircraft. They're so hot you can't wait to find a place for them in your latest idyll of love. The point being made here is this: the individual sounds—what some people call "ear candy"—may not work in your song. Use what you need, what is essential to the musical material at hand, and you'll produce a convincing, realistic track that really grooves.

The same principle applies to *any* sound you choose to play. If you have a great electric bass sound, think like a bass player. Pizzicato parts sound great with plucked strings, but they probably won't work as well with brass instruments, or sound as good. Use your musical smarts and you'll produce some very musical parts.

And remember: though you have a lot of tracks at your disposal in your MIDI sequencer, you don't have to use them all at once. Great arrangements employ space and distribute parts to various sections of an ensemble. Rarely does everybody play continuously throughout a piece of music. So think about that as you're laying down your tracks, and you'll avoid some problems at the mixing stage.

MIDI works for the arranger, then, in two ways. On the one hand, MIDI can provide the core materials for the performance itself—the instrumental sounds, the arrangement. The only thing you might need to add are some vocals (but even background voices can be MIDI-ized) and the occasional real instrument.

On the other, MIDI can allow you to give the musicians you work with a rough teaching track for their respective parts. A particular snap you want in the drums, a particular line you want on the bass: your MIDI recording can give your players the notes and the rhythms you're looking for. Your musicians just have to provide the feel.

For the rock/pop arranger, or any other serious composer MIDI recording offers unparalleled freedom and self-containment. The technology has never been more affordable or easier to use, and it gets cheaper and more user-friendly every day. The quality and variety of sounds available is staggering, and the best computer software is set up so that when you have that ethereal melody in your head at 3:00 in the morning, instead of moaning into a tape recorder and hoping you can decipher it the next day, you can play it into your computer exactly as you hear it and save it. You won't hear an approximation the next day; you'll hear exactly what roused you from your sleep, waiting to be developed into your next hit. MIDI recording offers you the ideal capability of composing, arranging, performing, and recording your work without leaving your home, and the equipment does not require the larger, more specialized type of space that conventional tape recording usually calls for.

This is by no means everything that can be said about MIDI or the incredible things it allows you to do. At best, for reasons of space, we can only give you an overview of how MIDI involves an entirely different approach to the whole matter of making music. This is, after all, a book about rock arranging. Through the combination of digitalized sound, computers, and software programs, you can create an arrangement that is as big as the Rockies or as small as a hangnail.

We have also tried to look at some of the temptations MIDI can place in your musical life. The song, the lyric, the style you're working in: These are the things that should really determine how you use MIDI. You've got a million sounds lurking in those synthesizers and a million more ways of putting them together. Not every tune you arrange this way has to end up sounding like an outtake from *Sgt. Pepper's*. The thankful thing with MIDI is that even if you go overboard every once in a while, you can always change it. MIDI gives you the freedom to experiment and discover new instrumental sounds and colors in a way that is a lot less painful than bringing together a bunch of musicians and wasting everybody's time—including your own.

If you are really cued into a particular style of rock, try to use that style as your experimental starting point. How can you generate a sound digitally that sounds like eight million screaming Stratocasters? How do you duplicate the beat of the style?

The point with MIDI and synthesizers generally is that your song doesn't have to sound weird; it has to sound *right*, and it is really the tradition of the style—and every style, including punk thrashing-guitars-in-the-dead-of-night music—has a tradition of aesthetic underlying its style, that helps you find the focus of what you do with your computer and synthesizer in arranging your work.

Getting Started

If you don't have a computer at home, though, we thought we'd include a brief guide on the four basic computer systems and how they've been used to deal with making music. We've also included some information about sequencing software. We're trying not to take sides here, because every system has its advantages and disadvantages.

We've talked about the cost-effectiveness and the self-containment of the computer-based sequencing studio. Your computer is essentially a full production center, the basis of your MIDI recording operation. Let's see what your initial investment is going to be and what kinds of products you're going to get for your money.

There are four leaders in the computer world and they all offer a variety of advantages and disadvantages to the MIDI musician. They are: the IBM PC (personal computer) and PC compatibles, the Apple MacIntosh, the Atari series, and the Commodore Amiga.When we look at a computer as a prospective purchase with musical applications in mind, we should have two immediate concerns (besides the price)—the environment and the software support of that particular brand.

By "environment" we mean the appearance of the working system as we watch the monitor. Is there a lot of text to be read,or do we instead see a lot of pictures? Does the system seem heavily keyboard-reliant (the computer's keyboard, that is) or do we have to spend a lot of our time pointing and clicking with a mouse? Does the computer itself seem easy to use,or are we mystified and confused by its methods of operation?

These are all very important considerations because it is of primary importance that we are able to relax around our computers. The environment you feel most comfortable working in should determine your choice. The easier it is for you to use and understand, the more you'll get out of it. We can't overemphasize this point: only you can decide which computer feels best! If you speak to four different computer owners you'll almost invariably find that each thinks his or her particular brand is the best, most reliable, and easiest to use, as well as being the quickest and most powerful.

Their enthusiasm is usually based on the quality of the software available for the computer as much as the computer itself. The four leading computer manufacturers are by now well-supported by music software companies that write programs covering the full musical gamut. Sequencers for composition and performance, editor-librarians that enable you to reprogram sounds in your synths and then save and download them at will from your computer (great stuff entirely; you can store thousands of sounds using your computer's memory), and notation and transcription programs that enable you to score your music using traditional music notation and then print out that music for publication or rehearsal purposes.

So, in many respects, a computer is only as useful as the software written for it, and that's an important consideration for the prospective owner. Well-written software generally combines ease of use with a symbiotic relationship with the computer and should be judged accordingly. The more time you have to spend with a manual in your hand the less time you have to compose and play, so a powerful sequencing program with a confusing user interface is rather useless, however ingenious it may be.

Symbiosis refers to the harmony and mutual benefit that living beings enjoy with their environment. This is a useful description of good musical software. A good program is not only powerful and easy to use,but also takes advantage of the operating system and environment of the"host" it's written for. That means greater speed and efficiency in the creative process, and better control of the final product.

Let's take a look at the Big Four and see what you get for your dollar.

IBM PC and PC compatibles:

Price Range: $750 to $4,000, depending on the system you choose. Music software, anywhere from $80 to $400. MIDI interface: $100 to $160, depending on features and manufacturer.

IBM introduced the personal computer in the early 1980s. The original units were a complete package featuring the CPU (Central Processing Unit, the computer itself), a monitor, and a keyboard. They offered great resolution,meaning clarity of text and images on the monitor screen, and questionable graphics, meaning that pictorial images were often clumsy and somewhat primitive.

The graphics problem has since improved immeasureably, and the wide variety of screen resolution cards and monitors makes the IBM a very expandable system. You can "hotrod" a basic system according to your needs, increasing the running memory, adding disk drives, and so on, according to your budget.

IBM also licensed its operating system called DOS (Disk Operating System) from a third party software developer called Microsoft Inc. Microsoft wrote the software system of commands that essentially runs the computer. This delegation of responsibility left the IBM engineers better able to concentrate on and perfect the hardware problems that accompanied the design and production of this innovative home computer. It was a successful marriage of convenience, and the IBM PC was and is a tremendously popular and profitable unit.

It also led to the rise of a host of PC imitators who manufacture computers that mimic the appearance and environment of a true IBM at often half the price. IBM apparently couldn't care less, having already licensed most of its environment to someone else, and the consumer for once really benefits. When you buy a true IBM you pay for the name; a quality clone offers identical performance, features, and expandibility for far less money.

The compatibility of the computer is a big question since an unscrupulous manufacterer can support one or two pieces of software and claim IBM compatibility. Most, fortunately, are legitimate, and in terms of speed and performance versus dollars spent, PCs and compatibles deserve a good look.

Initially neglected by music software developers, the IBM is now enjoying a proliferation of music software. There are now a total of 28 sequencing programs available for the IBM as well as a big selection of notation and editor-librarian software.

The best sequencers use the IBM keyboard very effectively and sparingly so that typing the first letter of a command word, such as R for Record or N for Note will activate the desired response immediately. The cursor and value keys enable you to move around so you don't have to be an expert typist to utilize these programs' speed and power. Symbiosis at work. You can also use the mouse, if pointing and clicking is your thing, with most of these programs, though this option is often redundant in view of the efficiency of the keyboard control. Again, it's your choice.

The MIDI interfaces available generally offer one IN and two OUTS. These are the ports that connect the computer to the MIDI keyboards and enable the data stream to flow. They often read and write SMPTE code (an essential element in combining MIDI recording in the professional studio) or SYNC tone, and send a metronome audio "click" output that helps you play in time when you're recording. Roland, Voyetra, and Musicquest are some name brands to look for.

Sequencers vary from entry level "fun packages" that function as an introduction to MIDI recording to the most professional and sophisticated programs currently available. Twelve Tone Systems, Passport, Voyetra, and Dr.T's are but some of the developers writing quality affordable programs that run the musical gamut from sequencing to visual sound editing. Most programs support both monochrome (black and white or amber) and color, and you always have a choice when you buy a system as to which type of monitor and card you prefer.

The IBM and compatible systems amount to a comprehensive cost-effective computer package you should definitely consider!

The Apple Macintosh:

Price Range: $1,200 to $4,500; MIDI interface: $120 to $400; software: $100 to $600.

Cute, cuddly, powerful, portable, and pricey, the MAC was the first to call itself the musicans' computer. Its so-called Icon-oriented environment was in fact partly developed by musicians, and the MAC was initially and might still be the best software supported "music computer." Heavily reliant on the mouse, and featuring an endless array of menus, pictures, and command options you point at, click, and drag around the screen, its creators have appealed to the child in all of us in an attempt to remove the chill and mystery from the computer's working environment. If the IBM offers a nononsense, text-oriented appearance, the MAC offers exactly the opposite presentation, right down to the smiling little computer that welcomes you on the screen when you turn the thing on.

Once you get used to the mouse, which is a coordination exercise in itself, most of what you accomplish on a MAC is comparatively independent of the keyboard. You look at the screen, pull down a menu selection, click on whatever you need to work with, and go to it. The graphics and screen resolution are very good, and if you can get past the rather tiny screen size of the smaller MACs, the portability factor tends to compensate.

The newer MAC II series is much bigger, however, but price is definitely an issue. MACs are expandible, but the peripherals (hard drives, cards, etc.) are expensive. You even pay extra for a keyboard! Apple is quite protective of the MAC environment and tends to discourage imitators by filing hefty lawsuits. So there are no MAC clones to encourage a little healthy price competition. And the price goes up. MAC ownership can be a bit of a prestige gig.

The software available for it is, however, abundant and state-of-the-art, as are MIDI interfaces. Mark of the Unicorn, Opcode, Passport, and Coda are among the developers supporting the MAC, and their products generally combine ease of use with very advanced professional capabilities, all operating in that charming environment.

Sequencing, notation, and visual sound editing are all fully and capably represented. Check it out.

The Atari Series:

Price: $850 to $2,500; MIDI interface and included software: $100 to $600.

The Atari, a.k.a. the musician's computer, a.k.a. the "poor man's MAC." A very popular, cost-effective computer dedicated to musical tasks and somewhat useless outside of that area. The working environment is very similar to that of a MAC (they were in fact sued by Apple). Atari software is heavily mouse-driven, and offers a MAC-like array of pulldown menus, pictures, (featuring a hilarious bee that indicates processing), and other friendly environmental traits. The CPU includes a keyboard, disk drive, and built-in MIDI interface, so you can save some money there. The monitor is extra, however: a big screen with questionable resolution. The Atari is very well supported by a variety of music software developers, and its limits as a computer does not seem to have discouraged musicians at all. If the icon-oriented environment sounds like a fun way to work, and you don't have any serious ambitions for your computer outside of musical applications, this computer might be good for you. The quality and quantity of software available for it is competitive with anything else on the market. Developers include Hybrid Arts, Dr.T's, Steinberg-Jones, and C-Lab. Sequencing, notation, and visual editing software is fully represented. A must for mouse enthusiasts on a budget.

The Commodore AMIGA series:

Price Range: $1,000 to $4,000; software: $100 to $300; MIDI interface: $150 to $200.

Owners of this neglected computer swear they purchased the best-kept secret on the market. Known for its superb graphics and great resolution, the Amiga series was introduced when Commodore was experiencing turmoil at the financial and administrative levels and was almost discontinued. Construed as the flagship of the Commodore line, which also makes PC compatibles and a low-cost music computer of its own, software developers initially found it confusing to write for, and a lot of crash-happy programs and bad press unfortunately resulted. The series (and the company) is back—new, improved, and expanded into one of the most sophisticated and versatile home computers around. The addition of an optional PC compatible program card enables it to support the vast selection of IBM software as well as its own small but steadily burgeoning roster of music programs.

Like the IBM, it is capable of multitasking, meaning that with sufficient running memory (RAM—Random Access Memory) you can work on a tune, edit a video, and print out sheet music at the same time without ever exiting any of those programs.

This computer will undoubtedly enjoy increasing support from music software developers in all areas, so it might be worth it to look at one.

You now have a general idea of what's available to you and what you should look for. You should remember that your computer is not merely a music production center in disguise but also a long-term business aid and adviser. You can type and print out labels for cassettes, charts for rehearsals, lead sheets for your songs, and list the vitals on all your fellow musicians and industry contacts. Cover letters for the tape, flyers for the band—the list goes on. If you keep in mind the long-term benefit you'll derive from not having to pay for these services and the increased musical productivity you'll experience, the computer is going to look like a very good deal.

Think of it the next time you run out of studio funds.

Appendix

More Rudiments of Music

Key Signatures

As with all rules, there are exceptions. Two deserve mention here as they have to do with *key signature*. Firstly, many lead sheets only place the key signature at the top of the piece (on the very first staff). Secondly, pieces with many accidentals are sometimes written with the key signature of no sharps and no flats (the key of C major, though some might say that there's no key signature at all). Transcriptions of jazz solos come to mind as examples of this.

Each key signature covers both a major and a minor key—each being the relative of the other. If you're a true rock musician, you may not need to count more than three of either the sharps or the flats, but for the sake of completeness, here is the cycle of sharps and flats in the major and minor keys. The "number" column in the chart below refers to the number of accidentals in the key signature.

Number	Major	Minor
0 #	C	A
1 #	G	E
2 #	D	B
3 #	A	F#
4 #	E	C#
5 #	B	G#
6 #	F#	D#
7 #	C#	A#
8 #	G#	E#
9 #	D#	B#

After this point, or so the theorists tell us, key signatures based on sharps get counterproductive. Don't despair, though: there are still the flats to fill those idle hours:

Number	Major	Minor
0♭	C	A
1♭	F	D
2♭	B♭	G
3♭	E♭	C
4♭	A♭	F
5♭	D♭	B♭
6♭	G♭	E♭
7♭	C♭	A♭
8♭	F♭	D♭
9♭	B♭♭	G♭

A few points to watch for (apart from the horror potential of trying to read a piece in G minor): The perceptive reader will note that as you add a sharp to the key signature, the key is raised a fifth. Similarly, as you add a flat, you raise the key a fourth.

   Add a fourth to a fifth and what do you get? No, not a ninth (which would seem logical) but an octave. To wit: E to B is a fifth; B to E above that is a fourth. In the same ruthless logic that allows theorists to taunt us with the possibility ofthe key of D# major (complete with nine sharps, even if there are only eight notes), what the system of sharps and flats in key signatures reveals is the mystery of the Circle of Fifths (otherwise known as the Circle of Fourths), which leads one through each of the twelve different pitches before the circle is complete:

Ascending in fifths:
C G D A E B F# C# G# (or A♭) D# (or E♭) A# (or B♭) E# (or F) B# (or C)

Ascending in fourths:
C F B♭ E♭ A♭ D♭ (or C#) G♭ (or F#) C♭ (or B) F♭ (or E) B♭♭ (or A) E♭♭ (or D) A♭♭ (or G) D♭♭ (or C)

   Now, it doesn't *look* as if either of the circles goes through the twelve pitches, but our music (as opposed to that of the Indian subcontinent, for example) involves an *enharmonic* system. That is to say, all pitches can carry different names, depending on which scale you're using. What is G# in the E major scale, for example, is essentially A♭ in the F minor scale. They are both the same note on the keyboard as well as on the guitar.

What this means for you as an arranger is that you can tell your musicians to play an A♭ minor chord, and what they can play for you is a G# minor chord and it will be a-okay.

This leads us to two accidentals not covered in the discussion of Example 14: the double sharp (which resembles an "×") and the double flat (♭♭). They are rare, but not all that rare, and are part of the logic of the musical system as it approaches absurdity.

Say you want to write out a B augmented chord. The augmented note is the fifth above the tonic—you raise it a half step above the natural fifth. The B major triad is spelled B-D#-F#; the B augmented triad is spelled B-D#-FX. Your fingers would fall, however, on the B, D#, and G notes on the keyboard.

In the case of the double flat, you find yourself trying to spell the Gb minor triad. To go from the major to the minor, you lower the third of the triad a half step. E major becomes E minor when you change the G# to G, for instance. In Gb, the major triad reads Gb -Bb -Db ; the minor triad, however, reads Gb -Bbb -Db .

If you find this all somewhat confusing, don't worry—it could always be worse. Try spelling a Cb diminished triad some time . . .

Dynamics

Dynamic marks indicate changes in the volume of the music. Dynamic marks can be expressed in either words or signs. If they come in the form of words (*crescendo*, for example) or abbreviations (*mp* or *ff*), they are always placed below the notes on the staff to which they refer. If they are used in terms of signs, they are located near the note head, either above or below the staff.

Word directions can become very long when written in the traditional Italian, so arrangers often use abbreviations (*dim*, *cresc*, etc.). The indications range from very soft to very loud.

The words *crescendo* for increasing in loudness (abbreviated as *cresc*) and *diminuendo* or *decrescendo* for gradually gettingsofter (*dim* and *decresc*, respectively) can be used alone or in conjunction with dynamic markings.

Accents and Attacks

Accent marks signify notes or chords to be accented. There are four different accent marks, and they may be placed above or below the notehead, depending upon where on the staff the notehead lies. When dealing with an entire phrase, however, most modern players prefer to have all of the accents marks placed in the same area, either above or below the staff. The most commonly seen accent mark looks like a small wedge (*marcato*). It directs one to play with a strong attack.

The same wedge turned 90 degrees in either direction becomes an accent mark denoting *sforzato*—to be played with a very strong attack. A *dot* means *staccato* or very short. A short line horizontal to the staff means *tenuto*; that is, it indicates a note that should be played with some attack and held for its full duration. *Marcato* and *sforzando* can be used with the dot and line. Here are four examples of such combinations:

> $\geq$: Full duration with strong attack
> $\geq$: Clipped with strong attack
> $\hat{\ }$: Full duration with very strong attack
> $\hat{:}$: Clipped with very strong attack

The *attack* describes the way in which the player first strikes the note or the chord. A hard attack for a guitarist, for example, involves the full weight of the arm and the wrist against the string. A soft attack, on the other hand, is a very light stroke on the string.

If you find yourself writing for strings (and it could always happen), you may discover that the reason you want strings in the first place is the variety of attacks available with bowed instruments. That's the reason why string parts have some of their own terms, especially *pizzacato* (*pizz* for short), which tells the player to pluck the string with the finger. Phrase markings (see Example 14), however, tell the musician to play all the notes grouped in a phrase within a single sweep of the bow. The attack of the *pizz* is the opposite of the non-attack of a note played within a phrase.

If you want your guitarist to simulate the Nashville equivalent of the *pizz*, you should write "muted" at the top of the part. If he or she is lucky enough to have a Gretsch Country Gentleman, then all he or she has to do is flick a knob that presses a sponge pad against the strings; otherwise, what this instruction does is tell the player to rest the fleshy part of the picking hand against the strings. This absorbs the vibra-tions of the strings, giving the player that down-home *pizz* effect.

Alterations to the Clefs

Octave marks indicate that a musical section is to be played either an octave higher or lower than what is indicated on the staff. The symbol *8va* or simply *8* placed above the staff indicates that the passage encompassed by the broken line and bracket is to be played one octave higher than notated. You can see this in the keyboard part in Example 78, found in Chapter 5.

When the symbol *8va bassa*, *8va* or *8* is placed beneath a passage, the music should be played an octave lower than written. All octave symbols are followed by a broken line and closed with a bracket. Octave signs should not be used unnecessarily, but only in cases of very extreme range or limited space. They are especially useful when writing out guitar parts to be played very high up on the fingerboard.

For hard-minded theorists, the guitar should be notated with the G clef, it's true, but always with an accompanying *8va* mark at the bottom of the clef. The reason for this is that the guitar is not a soprano but a tenor instrument. Because it falls in a lower-middle range, it is a good rhythm instrument and is also well-suited for solo performance.

Polyphony

Counterpoint is defined as music consisting of two or more melodic lines sounding simultaneously. But when we talk about the rhythmic counterpoint of R & B and funk music, we are really referring to two (or more) different *rhythmic* lines coexisting in musical time/space. This gives a bouncy, very danceable feel to the music, unlike the endless thud of the bass and drums in hard rock and metal.

In describing two or more independent melodic lines occurring at the same time, counterpoint is generally referring to melodies in different registers (soprano against the tenor, for example, or alto against the bass). Paul McCartney, with that tremendous melodic gift of his, is a pop master of melody and countermelody. The Roches are also terrific at this kind of thing —witness the title track to their album, *Speak*.

But if you want to hear some smoking counterpoint, check out a fugue by J.S. Bach some time. There, he takes one musical idea and plays with it among as many as five different parts. It's amazing how intense a simple melody can get in the right hands.

Drawing from Non-Western Sources in Your Arrangements

We generally think of modern music strictly in terms of our own musical system—major and minor scales, 4/4 time, and so on. Occasionally, we give a nod of the head to the North Africans and the Brazilians or the Aborigines of Australia or the Indians of the Andes Mountains, but somehow, we end up transforming their musical ideas into our own—not entirely unlike the colonists of the eighteenth century who went about the world claiming vast stretches of land for the enrichment of the home country. One faces the danger of explaining "one musical system in terms of another; to describe a non-diatonic music in diatonic terms."

Our tendency with the blues scale is to think of it as the European scale without a couple of notes. But it has been suggested that the Africans were not using a diatonic scale lacking a fourth and seventh interval. Instead, their scale consisted of five intervals, roughly equivalent to the Western pentatonic scale.

The same might be said in the matter of hearing a recording of a Trinidad guitarist. To our ears, such ethnic recordings often sound "out of tune," but it might be the case that it is not the guitar but our ears that aren't properly aligned.

The point in all of this is that you can, like Peter Gabriel, George Harrison, and even Keith Richards, learn from non-Western styles and use them in your work. But don't be surprised if you have trouble writing them out in your arrangements. Our tuning system and our musical logic only work for Western music.

Patterns

The Harvard Brief Dictionary of Music defines *ostinato* as "a clearly defined melodic phrase which is persistently repeated, usually in the same voice part and at the same pitch, although in extended compositions it is sometimes transferred to another voice part or to another pitch." The *ostinato* technique has been widely used in jazz, especially boogie-woogie, in which the left hand plays a repeating bass line against which the right hand improvises.

We most often use ostinato figures in the bass, where they provide the foundation for the song, but it can also figure in the use of a meaty guitar riff, as in the Stones' "Last Time" or the Beatles' "Day Tripper."

In recent years, we have most often heard ostinato monotony in the relentless wash of New Age music—the logic being, no doubt, that if you don't like a pattern the first time around, maybe you'll groove to it after you've heard it 60 times over. It is with the arpeggiated ostinato pattern that the New Age style achieves its singularly hypnotic effect. No wonder some of those tapes bear the legend: "Warning! Do not listen to this when driving your car. May cause drowsiness and accidents." See the chapters on blues and rock for further details.

Singing Styles

Falsetto: This is a style of singing that involves strictly the upper registers of the voice, in the realm of the singer's notes after the breaking point in the vocal range. It is what they call in the trade a "head voice"—that is, it is produced in the throat rather than from the gut. Prince is a master of the falsetto in pop, but you will also find it often in high male harmonies.

Parlando is, as the Italian word implies, more of a spoken style of singing. Lou Reed is the great perpetrator of this approach, though Leonard Cohen, another great non-singer, is an avowed master. Generally, it is a useful effect if you want to emphasize the meaning of a lyric within the greater context of a song.

Sotto voce is a singing technique where the singer sings at a volume just above a whisper. The voice and the notes are full; it's the volume that is quiet. A good surprise to pop on your listeners every once in a while.

MIDI

Here is a rundown of some of the more important words, phrases, and materials circulating around synthesizer and computer-generated music:

MIDI (Musical Instrument Digital Interface): This is the system as a whole that allows synthesizers to talk to each other and allows the computer to govern the synthesizers. With the appropriate software (computer program), you can record (sequence) different voices and even generate scores for live musicians.

Controller: This is the synthesizer you use to drive the MIDI system.

Controller Card:This is the card you put in the back of your computer that allows you to connect it with one or more synthesizers.

RAM: Forget what this means in computerese. In English, this is the active working memory of the computer. Because sequencing and notation software programs often are very complicated (and the more user-friendly they are, the more memory they require to operate), the more RAM your computer has, the better it will be for this kind of work.

Hard Drive: The hard drive is a storage system in the computer that allows you to install a large program in the computer without having to spend your day pulling diskettes in and out of it all the time. It also allows you to store your recorded information in the machine—again without having to worry about diskettes.

Even if you have a hard drive, though, it is always a goodidea to keep back-ups of the work and the programs you store on the hard drive—hard drives have a way of crashing just when you think you've got them pegged.

Suggested Reading

Baraka, Amiri (Le Roi Jones). *Blues People*. New York: Quill, 1963. Essential reading for any serious student of the blues. Baraka gives a unique perspective on the continuing role of the Afro-American in creating today's musical styles.

The Beatles. *The Compleat Beatles* (two volumes). New York: Bantam Books, 1980. The complete Beatle recordings, lovingly transcribed and edited by Milton Okun. Though not fully orches-trated, these renditions of the Beatles' songs include all the parts of the songs, from Harrison's guitar fills to the French horn solo in "For No One."

Brunning, Bob. *Blues—The British Connection*. New York: Sterling Publishing Company, 1986. A kind of "who's who" of '60s British rock and blues. Great for fans of music trivia.

Gillett, Charlie. *The Sound of the City: The Rise of Rock 'n' Roll*. New York: Dell Publishing Co., 1972. One of the best histories of rock ever written. Where others fall into the trap of confusing opinion with fact, Gillett, trained as a sociolo-gist, gives some reasonable hows and whys about the development and popularity of rock up through 1969.

Kaye, Carol. *Electric Bass Lines No. 1*. New York: Warner Brothers Publications, 1982. A "hands-on" guide to creating effective bass lines in all of the contemporary styles by an acknowledged master of the instrument.

Kinder, Bob. *The Best of the First: The Early Days of Rock and Roll*. Chicago: Adams Press, 1986. A brief history of rock and its performers from the eye of a Missouri drummer/writer.

Michaels, Mark. *Rock Riffs for Guitar, Blues Riffs for Guitar, Heavy Metal Riffs for Guitar, New Wave Riffs for Guitar, and Rockabilly Riffs for Guitar*. New York: Music Sales Corporation, 1982. Useful books (companion audio and video-tapes are available from Riff Companion Series) which give hundreds of stylistic licks and embellishments in the five major rock genres.

Riddle, Nelson. *Arranged by Nelson Riddle*. New York: Warner Brothers Pub-lications, 1985. A very enjoyable book of stories and anecdotes from the noted arranger of Frank Sinatra, Linda Ronstadt, Ella Fitzgerald, etc.

Sandole, Adolph. *Arranging and Harmony for Stage Band*. New York: Adolph Sandole, 1982. Just what the title says.

Sebesky, Don. *The Contemporary Arranger*. Sherman Oaks: Alfred Publish-ing Company, 1984. The Bible for serious arrangers. An in-depth analysis of arranging for all instruments, mostly in the area of jazz. Not to be missed by any student of arranging.

Stokes, Geoffrey. *Starmaking Machinery*. New York: Pantheon Books, 1976. The experiences of Commander Cody and His Lost Planet Airmen at the hands of the now-defunct ABC record label and Warner Brothers will fill you with as much horror as any low-budget terror film. Stokes provides extraordinary insight into the operations of the music industry.

Tobler, John and Grundy, Stuart. *The Record Producers*. New York: St. Mar-tin's Press, 1982. Stories and anecdotes of well-known record producers/arrangers/engineers who have shaped the sound of rock music (Phil Spector, Mickey Most, Tony Visconti, etc.).

Williams, Ken J. *Music Preparation: A Guide to Music Copying*. New York: Ken J. Williams Publications, 1980. An invaluable aid to the musician/arranger who wants to prepare professional-looking charts and scores by hand.

About the Authors

Mark Michaels has been playing guitar since age 9 and teaching music for fifteen years. This is his ninth book on music instruction. He founded Riff Companion Series in 1984 to market the line of audio and video tapes which correspond to his "Riff Series." An accomplished guitarist, arranger and producer, Mark presently teaches guitar at the American Institute of Guitar. He lives in the New York area with his wife, Kathy and dog, Goldy.

Jackson Braider, a graduate in Music History from SUNY/Buffalo, has been writing about music and musicians for the past fifteen years. An editor of *Fast Folk Musical Magazine,* he has contributed frequently to a variety of professional musicians' magazines, including *Acoustic Guitar, Frets, Keyboard, Billboard,* and *The Classical Guitarist.* When not writing about music, he is often playing it, not only as a singer/songwriter, but as an assistant guitarist at the Cathedral of St. John the Divine in New York City. Currently, he is at work on a biography of Johann Sebastian Bach.